SPANISH WORDLIST

T. Murray

*Head of Modern Languages,
Edgecliff School, Staffordshire
Chief Examiner in Spanish (MEG)*

CASSELL

Cassell Publishers Ltd
Villiers House,
41-47 Strand,
London,
WC2N 5JE

First published 1989
Reprinted 1990, 1991

ISBN 0-304-31622-9

**British Library Cataloguing in Publication
Data**

Murray, T.
  Cassell's Spanish wordist
  1. Spanish language. Spanish & English
  dictionaries
  I. Title
  463'.21

Typeset in Century Schoolbook by Witwell Ltd
Printed in Great Britain by Courier International Ltd,
Tiptree, Essex

Dedication

To my mother and to the memory of my father

To the Teacher, Pupil and Parent

All the GCSE boards have issued vocabulary lists on which they will base their exams. No questions may be asked which require knowledge of words not on the lists.

Unfortunately, no English translation is provided with these lists and this leaves teachers in a quandary as to how to exploit them. In fact, it has been the incessant demands from my pupils for a translation that has caused me to write this book.

This GCSE vocabulary book is based on the vocabulary lists provided by the GCSE exam boards. It has been structured to cover the vocabulary lists of each and every board and the requirements of Standard Grade. Very simple words, unlikely words and some words which are the same in English have been omitted; a few similar or identical words appear in the English/Spanish list but not the Spanish/English.

We are now being forced to use a number of different books to cover the four skill areas of listening, speaking, reading and writing. Few (if any) have a comprehensive Spanish/English and English/Spanish vocabulary list. Few (if any) of the major coursebooks have such a list. I am sure that GCSE and Standard Grade students of all ages will find this book a valuable companion as it provides both.

Space has been provided for any additional words that you might like to insert. Words like 'match' have been contextualized so that you know whether you are referring to a football match or a match for lighting a fire.

There is a section at the front covering numbers, days, months, seasons, time and weather.

¡Suerte!

T. Murray
Head of Modern Languages, Edgecliff School, Staffs,
Chief Examiner in Spanish (MEG)

Numbers

Cardinal numbers

Los números

Los números cardinales

0	cero	40	cuarenta
1	uno, una	50	cincuenta
2	dos	60	sesenta
3	tres	70	setenta
4	cuatro	80	ochenta
5	cinco	90	noventa
6	seis	100	cien/ciento (cien días
7	siete		cien pesetas)
8	ocho	101	ciento uno
9	nueve	110	ciento diez
10	diez	199	ciento noventa y nueve
11	once	200	doscientos, -as
12	doce	300	trescientos, -as
13	trece	400	cuatrocientos, -as
14	catorce	500	quinientos, -as
15	quince	600	seiscientos, -as
16	dieciséis	700	setecientos, -as
17	diecisiete	800	ochocientos, -as
18	dieciocho	900	novecientos, -as
19	diecinueve	1,000	mil
20	veinte	1,100	mil cien
21	veintiuno	2,000	dos mil
22	veintidós	100,000	cien mil
30	treinta	1,000,000	un millón (un millón
31	treinta y uno		pesetas)

Ordinal numbers

Los números ordinales

first	el primero
second	el segundo
third	el tercero
fourth	el cuarto
fifth	el quinto
sixth	el sexto
seventh	el séptimo
eighth	el octavo
ninth	el noveno
tenth	el décimo
eleventh	el undécimo
twelfth	el duodécimo

The days of the week	Los días de la semana
Sunday	domingo
Monday	lunes
Tuesday	martes
Wednesday	miércoles
Thursday	jueves
Friday	viernes
Saturday	sábado
today	hoy
yesterday	ayer
tomorrow	mañana
the day before yesterday	anteayer
the day after tomorrow	pasado mañana
the day before	la víspera
the next day	al día siguiente
on Monday	el lunes
on Fridays	los viernes
every Saturday	cada sábado
in the morning	por la mañana
in the evening/ afternoon	por la tarde
at night	de noche, por la noche

Note: no capital letter for days of the week in Spanish

The months of the year	Los meses del año
January	enero
Feburary	febrero
March	marzo
April	abril
May	mayo
June	junio
July	julio
August	agosto
September	se(p)tiembre
October	octubre
November	noviembre
December	diciembre

What is the date today?	¿ Qué día es hoy?
Today is/it's Monday the 13th of January (1992)	Hoy es el lunes, trece de enero (mil novecientos noventa y dos)
Sunday the 1st of May	Domingo el primero de mayo
The second of May	El dos de mayo

Note: the cardinal numbers – see above – are used i
Spanish for dates from 2nd to 31st

The seasons / Las estaciones

spring	primavera (*f*)
summer	verano (*m*)
autumn	otoño (*m*)
winter	invierno (*m*)
in spring/ in the spring	en la primavera

The time / La hora

What's the time? What time is it?	¿Qué hora es?
What time do you make it?	¿Qué hora tienes?
It's one o'clock	Es la una
It's four o'clock	Son las cuatro
It's five past four	Son las cuatro y cinco
It's a quarter past six	Son las seis y cuarto
It's half past eight	Son las ocho y media
It's ten to six	Son las seis menos diez
It's a quarter to three	Son las tres menos cuarto
half an hour	media hora
a quarter of an hour	un cuarto de hora

at about four o'clock	a eso de las cuatro
it's exactly seven o'clock	son las siete en punto
it's just after two o'clock	son las dos y pico
at midday	a mediodía
at midnight	a medianoche
at dawn	al amanecer
at dusk	al caer la tarde, al atardecer
at nightfall	al caer la noche, al anochecer
At 16.25	A la dieciséis veinticinco
At 14.45	A las catorce cuarenta y cinco
At 18.00	A las dieciocho (horas)
At 10 a.m.	A las diez de la mañana
At 4 p.m.	A las cuatro de la tarde
At 11 p.m.	A las once de la noche

The weather / El tiempo

What's the weather like?	¿Que tiempo hace?
It's hot/cold	Hace calor/frío
It's sunny/windy	Hace sol/viento
It's raining/ snowing	Está lloviendo/ nevando
It's frosty	Hay escarcha
It's misty/foggy	Hay neblina/niebla
The weather's fine/bad	Hace bien tiempo/ mal tiempo

a eso de la una	about one o'clock
abajo	downstairs
el abanico	fan (lady's)
la abeja	bee
abierto	open
el abogado	lawyer
el abonado	subscriber
abrazar 73	to embrace
el abrazo	embrace
el abrebotellas	bottle-opener
el abrelatas	tin-opener
el abrigo	coat
abrir 5	to open
abrocharse el cinturón	to fasten your seat-belt
¡en absoluto!	absolutely not!
el abuelo/la abuela	grandfather/mother
aburrido	bored, boring
aburrirse 5	to be bored
acabar 3	to finish
acabar de (comer)	to have just (eaten)
acampar 3	to camp
el acantilado	cliff
el acceso (de tos)	fit (of coughing)
la acción	action
el aceite	oil
la aceituna	olive
el acento	accent
aceptar 3	to accept
la acera	pavement
el acero	steel
acerca de	about (concerning)
acercarse 7/	to approach
acompañar 3	to accompany
el aire acondicionado	air-conditioning
aconsejar 3	to advise

acordarse *19*	to remember
acostarse *19*	to go to bed
acostumbrado	accustomed
la actividad	activity
el actor/la actriz	actor/actress
actualmente	at present
hacer el esquí acuático	to go water-skiing
acudir a (una cita) *5* ⌐ *to rush*	to go to (an appointment)
el acuerdo	agreement
de acuerdo	agreed
adelantado	advanced
adelantar *3*	to overtake
¡adelante!	forward!
además	besides
además de	in addition to
adentro	inside
adiós	goodbye
admitir *5*	to admit
¿adónde?	where to?
adquerir *uirir 30*	to acquire
la aduana	customs (-office)
el aduanero	customs officer
el adulto	adult
afeitarse *3*	to shave
la afición	hobby
el aficionado	enthusiast
afortunadamente	fortunately
afortunado	fortunate
afuera	outside
las afueras	outskirts
agarrar *3*	to seize
la agencia de viajes	travel agent
la agenda	notebook; diary
agitado	agitated

agitar (el pañuelo)	to wave (your handkerchief)
agotado	exhausted
agotarse	to run out of
agradable	pleasant
agradecer	to thank for
agradecido	grateful
la **agricultura**	agriculture
la **agua**	water
la **agua** mineral (con gas)	mineral water (fizzy)
el **agua** mineral (sin gas)	mineral water (still)
el **aguacate**	avocado
el **aguacero**	rainstorm
aguantar	to put up with
aguardar	to wait for
el **aguardiente**	brandy
agudo	sharp
la **aguja**	needle
el **agujero**	hole
ahí	there
ahogarse	to drown
ahora	now
por **ahora**	for the moment
ahorrar	to save (money)
estar al **aire** libre	to be in the open air
aislado	isolated
el **ajedrez**	chess
el pollo al **ajillo**	chicken in garlic
el **ajo**	garlic
una señal de **alarma**	alarm signal
el **albañil**	bricklayer
el **albaricoque**	apricot
el **albergue**	lodging

el **albergue** juvenil	youth hostel
la **albóndiga**	meatball
la **alcachofa**	artichoke
el **alcalde**	mayor
el **alcázar**	fortress
la **aldea**	village
el **aldeano**	villager
alegrarse 3	to be happy
alegre	happy
la **alegría**	happiness
alejarse 3	to go away
alemán/Alemania (f)	German/Germany
el **alfiler**	pin
la **alfombra**	carpet
la **alfombrilla**	rug
algo	something
algo (pequeño)	rather (small)
el **algodón**	cotton
alguien	someone
alguno	some
la **alhaja**	jewel
el **alimento**	food
alimentos congelados (m)	frozen food
el **almacén**	shop
los grandes **almacenes**	big shops
la **almeja**	clam
la **almohada**	pillow
almorzar 74	to lunch
el **almuerzo**	lunch
el **alojamiento**	lodgings
alojarse 3	to take lodgings
el **alpinismo**	climbing
el/la **alpinista**	climber
alquilar 3	to hire
el **alquiler**	rent

alrededor de	around
los alrededores	area around
alto	high
¡alto!	stop!
la altura	height
el alumno/la alumna	pupil
allá	there
allí	there
la ama de casa	housewife
amable	pleasant
amargo	bitter
amarillo	yellow
la ambición	ambition
ambicioso	ambitious
el ambiente	atmosphere
ambos	both
amenazar 73	to threaten
América del Sur (f)	South America
el amigo/la amiga	friend
la amistad	friendship
amistoso	friendly
el amo	boss master
el amor	love (nn)
amueblado	furnished
anciano	old
ancho	wide
andar 59	to walk
el andén	platform (on station)
el anfiteatro	balcony (in cinema)
el anillo	ring (on finger)
dibujos animados (m)	cartoons
animar 3	to encourage
¡ánimo!	cheer up!
anoche	last night
el ante	suede

anteayer	the day before yesterday
anterior *preceding*	previous
antes	before
antiguo	ancient
antipático	unpleasant
anublado	cloudy
anunciar 3	to announce
el **anuncio**	advertisement
añadir 5	to add *in speaking*
el **año**	year
el **año** pasado	last year
el **año** próximo (que viene)	next year
apagar 72	to switch off (e.g. a light)
el **aparador**	sideboard
¡Al **apartato**!	speaking! (on phone)
el **aparcamiento**	car park
aparcar 71	to park
aparecer 35	to appear
el **apartamento**	apartment
el **apellido**	surname
apenas	scarcely
el **aperitivo**	aperitif
apetecer 35	to take your fancy
la **aplicación**	studiousness
apreciar 3	to appreciate
aprender 4	to learn
el **aprendiz**	apprentice
aprobar 19	to pass (an exam)
¡Qué **aproveche**!	enjoy your meal!
aproximadamente	approximately
aproximarse 3	to approach
el **apunte**	note (e.g. in a notebook)

aquel/aquella	that
aquellos/aquellas	those
aquí	here
el árbitro	referee
el árbol	tree
arder	to burn
la arena	sand
argentino/Argentina (f)	Argentinian/ Argentina
armar (una tienda)	to put up (a tent)
el armario	wardrobe
el arquitecto	architect
la arquitectura	architecture
arrancar	to start (a car)
arreglar (la casa)	to tidy (the house)
arreglar (pinchazos)	to fix (punctures)
arriba	upstairs
arrojar	to throw
el arroz	rice
el arte	art
el pollo asado	roast chicken
asar	to roast
el ascensor	lift (elevator)
el asco	disgust
dar asco	to disgust
¡Qué asco!	How disgusting!
el aseo	toilet
asesinar	to murder
el asesinato	murder
¡así así!	so so!
así que	so that
el asiento	seat
la asignatura	subject (at school)
asistir	to be present at
asomarse	to look out (e.g. of window)

el **aspirador**; la **aspiradora**	vacuum-cleaner
asqueroso	disgusting
asustarse 3	to be frightened
atacar 71	to attack
el **ataque**	attack
atar 3	to tie
la **atención**	attention
atentamente	politely
el **aterrizaje**	landing (of a plane)
aterrizar 73	to land (a plane)
el **atletismo**	athletics
atónito	astonished
el parque de **atracciones**	amusement park
el **atraco**	hold-up (robbery)
atractivo	attractive
atrás	behind
atrasado	delayed
atravesar 11	to cross
atreverse 4	to dare
atropellar 3	to knock down
la **aula**	classroom
aumentar 3	to increase
aun	even
aún	still
aunque	although
el **auricular**	receiver (telephone)
ausente	absent
austriaco/Austria (f)	Austrian/Austria
el **autobús**	bus
el **autocar**	coach (vehicle)
el/la **automovilista**	driver
la **autopista**	motorway
el **autor**/la **autora**	author/ess
autorizado	allowed

el **autostop**	hitch-hiking
hacer **autostop**	to go hitch-hiking
el/la **autostopista**	hitch-hiker
primeros **auxilios** (*m*)	first aid
la **avenida**	avenue
la **aventura**	adventure
la **avería**	breakdown (mechanical)
averiado	broken down (mechanical)
averiarse 75	to break down (mechanical)
el **aviador**	pilot
el **avión**	plane
avisar 3	to warn
el **aviso**	notice
la **avispa**	wasp
ayer	yesterday
la **ayuda**	help
ayudar 3	to help
el **ayuntamiento**	town hall
la **azafata**	air hostess
la **azotea**	flat roof
el **azúcar**	sugar
azul	blue
el **azulejo**	tile

_____   _____
_____   _____
_____   _____
_____   _____
_____   _____

el **bacalao**	cod
el **bache**	pothole (in road)
el **bachillerato**	exam (pre-university)
la **bahía**	bay
bailar	to dance
el **baile**	dance
la **bajada**	descent
bajar	to go down
bajo	below
el **balcón**	balcony
el **baloncesto**	basketball
la **balonred**	netball
el **banco**	bank (in High Street); bench
la **bandeja**	tray
la **bandera**	flag
el **bañador**	swimming costume
bañarse	to bathe
baño	bath
el traje de **baño**	bathing costume
barato	cheap
la **barba**	beard
el **barco**	boat
dar un paseo en **barco de vela**	to go for a sail
la **barra**	loaf
barrer	to sweep
el **barrio**	district
el **barro**	mud
bastante	enough
bastar	to be enough
la **basura**	rubbish
el **basurero**	dustman
la **bata**	dressing gown

la **batería**	battery (in a car)
batir 5	to beat
el **baúl**	trunk (luggage)
el **bebé**	baby
beber 4	to drink
la **bebida**	drink
la **beca**	grant (e.g. for a student)
belga/Bélgica (*f*)	Belgian/Belgium
bello	beautiful
besar 3	to kiss
el **beso**	kiss
la **biblioteca**	library
la **bicicleta**	bicycle
bien	well
¡Qué **bien**!	How nice!
bienvenido	welcome
el **biftec**/el **bistec**	steak
el **bigote**	moustache
el **billar**	billiards
el **billete**	ticket
el **billete de banco**	banknote
el **billete de ida y vuelta**	return ticket
el **billete sencillo (de ida)**	single ticket
la **biología**	biology
el **bizcocho**	biscuit
blanco	white
la **blusa**	blouse
la **boca**	mouth
la **bocacalle**	side street
el **bocadillo**	sandwich
la **boda**	wedding
la **bodega**	cellar *wine shop*
la **boina**	beret
el **bolígrafo**	ballpoint
la **bolsa**	bag

el **bolsillo**	pocket
el **bolso** de mano	handbag
el **bombero**	fireman
la **bombilla**	bulb (light)
bonito	pretty
el **boquerón**	anchovy
a **bordo**	on board
borracho	drunk
la **borrasca**	storm
el **bosque**	wood (forest)
la **bota**	boot
la **botella**	bottle
el **botón**	button
las **bragas**	knickers
el **brazo**	arm (of body)
brillar 3	to shine
la **brisa**	breeze
británico	British
el **broche**	brooch
la **loción**	
bronceadora	suntan cream
broncearse 3	to tan (in the sun)
bueno	good
la **bujía**	candle
el **buque**	ship
el **burro**	donkey
buscar 7!	to look for
la **butaca**	armchair
el **buzón**	letter-box

_____ _____
_____ _____
_____ _____
_____ _____

el **caballero**	gentleman
el **caballo**	horse
el **cabello**	hair
la **cabeza**	head
la **cabina** telefónica	telephone box
al **cabo** de	at the end of
la **cabra**	goat
la **cacerola**	saucepan
cada	each
la **cadena**	chain; channel (on TV)
caer 50	to fall
el **café** con leche	coffee (white)
el **café** cortado	coffee (with some milk)
el **café** solo	coffee (black)
la **cafetera**	coffee pot
la **cafetería**	café
la **caja**	box
la **caja** (in supermarket)	checkout
la **caja** de ahorros	savings bank
el **cajero**	cashier
el **cajón**	box (large); drawer
el **calamar**	squid
el **calcetín**	sock
calcular 3	to calculate
la **calefacción**	heating
calentar //	to heat
la **calidad**	quality
caliente	hot
el **calor**	heat
hacer **calor**	to be hot weather
caluroso	hot
calvo	bald
los **calzoncillos**	underpants
callarse 3	to be quiet

la **calle**	street
la **calle** mayor	street (main)
la **callejuela**	street (small)
la **cama**	bed
guardar **cama**	to stay in bed
hacer la **cama**	to make the bed
la **cama** de matrimonio	double bed
la **cama** doble	double bed
la **cama** individual	single bed
la **cámara**	camera
el **camarero**	waiter
camas gemelas (*f*)	twin beds
cambiar	to change
el **cambio**	change
el **camino**	way
el **camión**	lorry
la **camioneta**	van
la **camisa**	shirt
la **campana**	bell (e.g. on a church)
el **campesino**	peasant
el **campeón**	champion
el **campeonato**	championship
hacer **camping**	to camp
ir de **camping**	to go camping
el **campo**	countryside
el **campo** (de deportes)	field (sports)
la **canción**	song
cansado	tired
el/la **cantante**	singer
cantar	to sing
llover a **cántaros**	to pour with rain
la **cantidad**	quantity
la **cantina**	canteen
la **caña**	glass of beer
la **caña** de pescar	fishing-rod

capaz	capable
la capital	the capital (city)
el capitán	captain
la cara	face
¡Caramba!	Gosh!
el caramelo	sweet
la cárcel	gaol
carcomido	decayed
cargar (una batería) 72	to charge (a battery)
el cariño	affection
cariñoso	affectionate
la carne	meat
el carnet de conducir	driving licence
el carnet de identidad	identity card
la carnicería	butcher's shop
el carnicero	butcher
caro	dear (expensive)
el carpintero	carpenter
la carrera Road Run 7	career RACE
la carretera	road (between towns)
el carrito	trolley (in supermarket)
la carta	letter
el cartel	poster
la cartera	briefcase
el cartero	postman
la casa	house
casado	married
casarse 3	to marry
casi	almost
castaño	brown (chestnut)
las castañuelas	castanets
castigar 72	to punish
el castigo	punishment
el castillo	castle

la **catedral**	cathedral
a **causa** de	because of
la **caza**	hunting
cazar 73	to hunt
la **cebolla**	onion
ceder el paso	to give way (at junction)
célebre	famous
la **cena**	evening meal
cenar 3	to eat (evening meal)
el **cepillo** (de dientes)	brush (toothbrush)
cerca de	near
cercano	nearby
el **cerdo**	pig
la **cereza**	cherry
la **cerilla**	match (for a fire)
cero	zero
cerrado	closed
la **cerradura**	lock
cerrar //	to close
cerrar con llave	to lock
la **cerveza**	beer
el **césped**	lawn
el **cesto**/la **cesta**	basket
el **ciclismo**	cycling
el/la **ciclista**	cyclist
ciego	blind
el **cielo**	sky
cien(to)	hundred
la **ciencia**	science
la **ciencia-ficción**	science fiction
la **cifra**	figure (number)
el **cigarillo**	cigarette
el **cigarro**	cigar
la **cima**	top (e.g. of hill)

el **cine**	cinema
el **cinturón**	belt
el **cinturón** de seguridad	safety-belt
el **circo**	circus
la **ciruela**	plum
la **cita**	appointment
la **ciudad**	city
el **ciudadano**	citizen
¡**Claro**!	Of course!
la **clase**	lesson
clásico	classic
el/la **cliente**	customer
el **clima**	climate
el **cobarde**	coward
el **cobayo**	guinea-pig
cobrar (dinero) 3	to receive (money)
el **cocido**	stew
la **cocina**	kitchen
la **cocina** de gas	gas cooker
la **cocina** eléctrica	electric cooker
la **cocina** española	Spanish cooking
cocinar 3	to cook
el **cocinero**	cook (i.e. the person)
el **coche**	car
el **coche-cama**	sleeping car (on a train)
el **coche-comedor** (restorán)	dining car (on train)
el **codo**	elbow
coger 84	to get; to grasp
el **cojín**	cushion
cojo	lame
la **cola** —	queue *Tail*
el **colchón**	mattress
la **colección**	collection
coleccionar 3	to collect
el **colegio**	school

colgar 61	to hang
la coliflor	cauliflower
la colina	hill
colocar 71	to place
el columpio	swing
el collar	necklace
el comedor	dining-room
comenzar 64	to begin
comer 4	to eat
el comerciante	trader
los comestibles	food
cometer 4	to commit
la comida	meal
la comisaría	police station
como	as
¿cómo?	how?
cómodo	comfortable
el compañero/la compañera	friend
la compañía	company
compartir 5	to share
completo	full
comprar 3	to buy
hacer compras	to go shopping
ir de compras	to go shopping
comprender 4	to understand
comprobar 19	to check
el computador	computer
¡está comunicando!	engaged (phone)
con	with
el concierto	concert
el concurso	competition
conducir 39	to drive
el conductor	driver
el conejo	rabbit

la **conferencia**	phone call; conference
el **congelador**	freezer
congelar 3	to freeze
conocer 37	to know (a person or place)
conseguir 68	to obtain
la **consigna**	left-luggage office
constipado	having a cold
construir 44	to build
contar 19	to tell (a story)
contener 15	to contain
contento	happy
la **contestación**	answer (*nn*)
contestar 3	to answer
continuar 76	to continue
contra	against
el **contrabandista**	smuggler
controlar 3	to check (passports); to control
convidar 3	to invite
la **copa**	drink (of liquor)
copiar 3	to copy
el **corazón**	heart
la **corbata**	tie (that you wear)
el **cordero**	lamb
corregir 67	to correct
correos (*m*)	post office
correr 4	to run
la **corrida** de toros	bullfight
corriente	running (water)
cortar 3	to cut
cortés	polite
la **cortina**	curtain
corto	short

la **cosa**	thing
la **cosecha**	harvest
coser	to sew
la **costa**	coast
costoso	expensive
la **costumbre**	custom
crear	to create
crecer	to grow
la tarjeta de **crédito**	credit card
creer	to believe
la **criada**	maid
el **crimen**	crime
el **criquet**	cricket
el **cruce**	crossroads
cruzar	to cross
el **cuaderno**	exercise book
el **cuadro**	picture
¿**cuál**?	which?
cuando	when
¿**cuánto**?	how much?
cuanto antes	as soon as possible
el **cuarto** (de hora)	quarter (of an hour)
el **cuarto**	room
el **cubierto**	knife, fork and spoon
el **cubo**	bucket
la **cuchara**	spoon
el **cuchillo**	knife
el **cuello**	neck
la **cuenta**	bill (in a cafe)
darse **cuenta**	to realize
el **cuero**	leather
el **cuerpo**	body
el **cuidado**	care
cuidar	to look after

la **culebra**	snake
la **culpa**	blame
cultivar	to grow (e.g. vegetables)
la **cumbre**	top (of a mountain)
el **cumpleaños**	birthday
el **cuñado**/la **cuñada**	brother (sister)-in-law
el **cura**	priest
el **curso**	course
cuyo	whose

_____   _____
_____   _____
_____   _____
_____   _____
_____   _____

los **champiñones**	mushrooms
el **champú**	shampoo
la **chaqueta**	jacket
charlar	to chat
el **cheque** de viajero	traveller's cheque
el **chico**/la **chica**	boy/girl
la **chimenea**	chimney
el **chiste**	joke
chocar con	to collide with
el **chófer**	driver
el **chorizo**	garlic sausage
el **chubasco**	shower (of rain)
la **chuleta**	chop
el **churro**	fritter

el **daño**	damage
dar	to give
debajo de	under
deber	to have to; to owe
los **deberes**	homework
débil	weak
decidir	to decide
decir	to say
el **dedo**	finger
dejar	to let (allow)
dejar un sitio	to leave (a place)
delante de	in front of
delgado	thin
el **delito**	offence
los **demás**	the rest (i.e. the remainder)
demasiado	too much
dentro de	inside
denunciar	to report to the police
el **departamento**	compartment (on train)
el/la **dependiente/-a**	shop assistant
el **deporte**	sport
el/la **deportista**	sportsman/woman
deportivo	sporting
el **depósito**	petrol tank
todo **derecho**	straight on
a la **derecha**	on the right
los **derechos** de aduana	customs duties
desafortunadamente	unfortunately
desagradable	unpleasant
desaparecer	to disappear
el **desastre**	disaster
desayunar	to breakfast
el **desayuno**	breakfast

descansar	to rest
el descanso	rest
describir 5	to describe
descubrir 5	to discover
desde	from
desear	to want
desempleado	unemployed
el desempleo	unemployment
desgraciadamente	unfortunately
desmayarse	to faint
desnudarse	to undress
desobedecer	to disobey
despacio	slowly
el despacho	office
despedirse 6	to say goodbye to
despegar	to take off (a plane)
el despertador	an alarm clock
despertarse	to wake up
después	after
el destino	destination
destrozar 13	to destroy
el desvío	detour
el detalle	detail
detenerse	to stop
detestar	to hate
detrás de	behind
devolver	to give back
el día	day
el diamante	diamond
diario	daily
la diarrea	diarrhoea
dibujar	to draw
el dibujo	drawing
los dibujos animados	cartoons
el diente	tooth
difícil	difficult

la **dificultad**	difficulty
¡**Dígame!**	Hello! (answering phone)
el **dinero**	money
Dios (*m*)	God
la **dirección**	direction; address
directo	through (train)
el **director**	headmaster
dirigirse	to head for
el **disco**	record (music)
distinto	different
divertido	funny
divertirse	to enjoy yourself
divorciado	divorced
doblar (la esquina)	to turn (the corner)
doble	double
la **docena**	dozen
doler	to hurt
el **dolor**	pain
el **domicilio**	residence
donde	where
dormir	to sleep
dormirse	to fall asleep
el **dormitorio**	bedroom
la **droga**	drug
la **ducha**	shower (bathroom)
la **duda**	doubt
dudar	to hesitate, doubt
me **duele** la cabeza	I have a headache
el **dueño**	owner
dulce	sweet
el **dulce**	sweet (e.g. for child)
durante	during
durar	to last
duro	hard
el **duro**	a five-peseta coin

echar	to throw
echar de menos	to miss (someone)
la **edad**	age
el **edificio**	building
la **educación**	education
el **ejercicio**	exercise
el **elefante**	elephant
elegir	to choose
la **embajada**	embassy
embarazada	pregnant
el **embotellamiento**	traffic jam
emocionante	moving (emotionally)
el **empaste**	filling (in tooth)
empezar	to begin
el **empleado**	employee
el **empleo**	job
la **empresa**	firm
empujar	to push
enamorado	in love
encantado	pleased to meet you
encantar	to delight
encender	to light
encima	above
encontrar	to find
encontrar a un amigo	to meet a friend
enfadarse	to get angry
la **enfermedad**	illness
la **enfermera**	nurse
enfermo	ill
enfrente	opposite
enhorabuena	congratulations
enojado	annoyed
enorme	enormous
la **ensalada**	salad
la **enseñanza**	education; teaching

enseñar	to teach
entender	to understand
entonces	then
la entrada	entrance
entrar	to enter
entre	between
entregar	to deliver
el entremés	starter (in a restaurant)
entretanto	meanwhile
enviar	to send
envolver	to wrap up
la época	period of time
el equipaje	luggage
el equipo	team
la equitación	horse-riding
equivocarse	to make a mistake
la escalera	stairs
el escaparate	shop window
la escarcha	frost
escocés/Escocia (f)	Scottish/Scotland
escoger	to choose
esconder	to hide
escribir	to write
escribir a máquina	to type
el escritor/la escritora	writer
escuchar	to listen
la escuela	school
ese/esa	that
el esfuerzo	effort
este/esta	this
esos/esas	those
la espalda	back (of your body)
español/España (f)	Spanish/Spain
los espárragos	asparagus
el espectáculo	show

el **espejo**	mirror
la sala **de**	
espera	waiting room
esperar	to hope
esperar un tren	to wait for a train
espeso	thick
las **espinacas**	spinach
el **esposo**/la **esposa**	husband/wife
el **esquí**	skiing
el **esquí** acuático	water-skiing
esquiar	to ski
la **esquina**	corner (outside)
la **estación**	station
la **estación** de autobuses	bus station
la **estación** del año	season of the year
la **estación** de servicios	service station
estacionar	to park
el **estadio**	stadium
los **Estados** Unidos	United States
el **estanco**	tobacconist (shop)
el **estanque**	pond
estar	to be
la **estatua**	statue
el **este**	the east
el **estómago**	stomach
estos/**estas**	these
estrecho	narrow
la **estrella**	star
el **estreno**	first performance
el/la **estudiante**	student
estudiar	to study
los **estudios**	studies
estupendo	splendid
estúpido	stupid
evitar	to avoid
exacto	accurate

el	**examen**	exam
la	**excursión**	outing
el	**éxito**	success
la	**explicación**	explanation
	explicar	to explain
el	**expreso**	express train
	extranjero	foreign
el	**extranjero**	abroad
	extraño	strange

la	**fábrica**	factory
	fabricar	to manufacture
	fácil	easy
la	**falda**	skirt
	falso	false
la	**falta**	lack
hace	**falta**	it is necessary
	faltar	to lack; to be absent
el	**faro**	headlight
la	**farmacia**	chemist (shop)
	fastidiar	to annoy
por	**favor**	please
la	**fecha**	date (of the month)
	feliz	happy
	femenino	feminine
	feo	ugly
la	**feria**	fair
el	**ferrocarril**	railway

el día **festivo**	holiday
la **ficha**	form
la **fiebre**	temperature (fever)
la **fiesta**	festival
la **fiesta** particular	party (get-together)
la **fila**	line
el **fin**	end
por **fin**	at last
el **fin** de semana	weekend
la **finca**	farm
a **fines** de	towards the end of
la **firma**	signature
firmar	to sign
la **física**	physics
flaco	thin
el **flan**	caramel custard
flojo	weak
la **flor**	flower
el **florero**	vase
el **folleto**	brochure
la **fonda**	inn
al **fondo**	at the far end
el **forastero**	outsider
la **forma**	shape
forzar	to force
la **foto**(grafía)	photo(graph)
el **fotógrafo**	photographer
fracasar	to fail
la **frambuesa**	raspberry
francés/Francia (*f*)	French/France
la **frase**	sentence (words)
fregar los platos	to wash the dishes
frenar	to brake
los **frenos**	brakes
la **frente**	forehead
la **fresa**	strawberry

fresco	fresh
hacer fresco	to be cool weather
frío	cold
frito	fried
la frontera	border
la frutería	fruit store
el frutero	fruit-seller
el fuego	fire
la fuente	fountain
fuera	outside
fuerte	strong
fumar	to smoke
no funciona	out of order
el fusil	rifle
el futbolista	footballer

_____   _____
_____   _____
_____   _____
_____   _____

ABCDEF**G**HIJKLMNOPQRSTUVWXY

las gafas	glasses
las gafas de sol	sunglasses
galés/Gales (f)	Welsh/Wales
la galleta	biscuit
la gallina	hen
la gamba	prawn
el gamberro	hooligan
ganar	to win
ganarse la vida	to earn your living
el garaje	garage
garantizar	to guarantee

la **garganta**	throat
la **gaseosa**	lemonade
la **gasolina**	petrol
la **gasolinera**	petrol station
gastar	to spend (money)
los **gastos**	expense
el **gato**	cat
el **gazpacho**	soup (cold)
el **gemelo**	twin
por lo **general**	in general
la **gente**	people
el **gerente**	manager
la **gimnasia**	gymnastics
el **gimnasio**	gym (place)
el **gobierno**	government
el **golpe**	blow
golpear	to hit
la **goma**	rubber
gordo	fat
la **gorra**	cap
la **gota**	drop
gracias	thank you
gracioso	funny
la **gramática**	grammar
el **gramo**	gram(me)
la **Gran** Bretaña	Great Britain
grande	big
la **granja**	farm
el **granjero**	farmer
gratis	free (no charge)
gratuito	free (no charge)
grave	serious
griego/Grecia (f)	Greek/Greece
el **grifo**	tap
la **gripe**	influenza
gris	grey

gritar	to shout
la grúa	crane
grueso	thick
el grupo	group
el guante	glove
guapa	pretty
guapo	handsome
guardar	to keep
el guardarropa	wardrobe
el guardia	policeman
la **Guardia** Civil	civil guard
la guerra	war
el guía	guide (person)
la guía	guide (book)
la guía telefónica	telephone book
los guisantes	peas
la guitarra	guitar
gustar	to please
el gusto	taste

_____ _____
_____ _____
_____ _____
_____ _____

ABCDEFG**H**IJKLMNOPQRSTUVWXYZ

la haba	bean
haber + haber de	to have
hábil	clever, skillful
la habitación	room
la habitación doble	double room
la habitación individual	single room
la habitación libre	room available

el **habitante**	inhabitant
hablador	talkative
hablar	to talk
¡ni **hablar**!	unthinkable!
hace buen tiempo	it is good weather
hace dos años	two years ago
hace falta	it is necessary
hacer	to do
hacer caso	to take notice
hacer punto	to knit
hacer ruido	to make noise
hacia	towards
hallar	to find
la **hambre**	hunger
la **hamburguesa**	hamburger
la **harina**	flour
harto	fed up
hasta	until
hasta luego	goodbye
hay	there is; there are
hay que	it is necessary
el **helado**	ice-cream
helar	to freeze
la **herida**	wound
herido	injured
herir 27	to injure
el **hermano**/la **hermana**	brother/sister
hermoso	beautiful
hervir 27	to boil
el **hielo**	ice
la **hierba**	grass
el **hierro**	iron (metal)
papel **higiénico**	toilet paper
el **higo**	fig
el **hijo**/la **hija**	son/daughter
el **hilo**	thread

hinchado	swollen
hincharse	to swell
la **historia**	history; story
el **hogar**	home
la **hoja**	leaf
la **hoja** de papel	sheet of paper
hola	Hello
la **holandés/** **Holanda** (f)	Dutch/the Netherlands
el **hombre**	man
el **hombre** de negocios	businessman
el **hombro**	shoulder
la **hora**	hour
la **hora** punta	rush hour
el **horario**	timetable
la **horchata**	drink made from almonds
el **horno**	oven
hoy	today
la **huelga**	strike (stopping work)
el **hueso**	bone
el **huésped**	guest
el **huevo**	egg
huir	to run away
húmedo	damp
el **humo**	smoke

el carnet de identidad	identity card
identificar	to identify
el idioma	language
la iglesia	church
igual	same
el imbécil	fool
impedir	to prevent
el impermeable	raincoat
no importa	it doesn't matter
la importancia	importance
el impuesto	tax
incapaz	incapable
el incendio	fire
incluido	included
incluso	even
incómodo	uncomfortable
indicar	to point
la cama individual	single bed
infantil	childlike
informarse	to get information
los informes	information
el ingeniero	engineer
inglés/Inglaterra (f)	English/England
injusto	unjust
inmediatamente	immediately
inmenso	immense
inmóvil	motionless
inquietarse	to worry
la insolación	sunstroke
el instituto	school
intentar	to try
el intercambio	exchange
el interés	interest
interesarse en	to be interested in
introducir (monedas)	to insert (coins)

inútil	useless
el invierno	winter
el invitado	guest
la inyección	injection
ir	to go
irlandés/Irlanda (f)	Irish/Ireland
irse	to go away
la isla	island
italiano/Italia (f)	Italian/Italy
IVA (impuesto sobre el valor añadido)	VAT
a la izquierda	to the left

---

el jabón	soap
jamás	never
el jamón	ham
el jardín	garden
la jardinería	gardening
el jardinero	gardener
la jaula	cage
el jefe	chief, boss
el jerez	sherry
¡Jesús!	Bless you! (on sneezing)
joven	young
la joya	jewel

la **joyería**	jeweller's
jubilado	retired
jubilarse	to retire
las **judías**	beans
el **juego**	game
el **juez**	judge
jugar	to play
el **jugo**	juice
el **juguete**	toy
junto a	next to
jurar	to swear
justo	correct
el albergue **juvenil**	youth hostel
el club de **juventud**	youth club
juzgar	to judge

el **kilo**	kilogram(me)

el **labio**	lip
el día **laborable**	working day
al **lado** de	beside
el **ladrón**	thief
el **lago**	lake
la **lágrima**	tear (in your eye)
la **lámpara**	lamp

la **lana**	wool
la **langosta**	lobster
la **langostina**	prawn
lanzar 73	to throw
el **lápiz**	pencil
largo	long
a lo **largo** de	along
¡Qué **lástima**!	What a pity!
la **lata**	tin (can)
el **lavabo**	washbasin
la **lavadora** automática	washing-machine
el **lavaplatos**	dishwasher
lavar	to wash
lavarse	to wash yourself
la **lección**	lesson
la **lectura**	reading
la **leche**	milk
la **lechería**	dairy
el **lechero**	milkman
la **lechuga**	lettuce
leer	to read
la **legumbre**	pulse (e.g. beans)
lejano	distant
lejos de	far from
la **lengua**	tongue
la **lengua** viva	language (modern)
el **lenguado**	sole (fish)
lento	slow
lentamente	slowly
las **lentillas**	lenses (contact)
el **león**	lion
la **letra**	letter (of alphabet)
el **letrero**	notice (i.e. a sign)
levantarse	to get up
la **libertad**	liberty
la **libra** (esterlina)	pound (sterling)

libre	free
al aire libre	in the open air
la librería	bookshop
la libreta	notebook
el libro	book
el licenciado	graduate
el líder	leader
ligero	light (not heavy)
la limonada	lemonade
el limpiabotas	shoeshine boy
los limpiaparabrisas	windscreen wipers
limpiar	to clean
limpio	clean (adj)
lindo	pretty
la línea	line
la linterna	torch
la liquidación	bargain sale
estar listo	to be ready
ser listo	to be clever
el litro	litre
la localidad	seat (e.g. in a cinema)
la loción bronceadora	suntan cream
loco	mad
lograr	to manage (to do something)
Londres (m)	London
la lonja	slice (of meat)
la lucha	struggle
luchar	to fight
luego	then
el lugar	place
tener lugar	to take place
el lujo	luxury
el hotel de lujo	luxury hotel

la **lumbre**	fire (hearth)
la **luna**	moon
la **luna** de miel	honeymoon
la **luz**	light

_____   _____
_____   _____
_____   _____
_____   _____
_____   _____

_____

ABCDEFGHIJK**LL**MNOPQRSTUVWXY

la **llamada**	call; phone call
llamar	to call
llamar por teléfono	to phone
llamarse	to be called
llano	flat (e.g. pancake)
la **llave**	key
la **llegada**	arrival
llegar	to arrive
llegar a	to manage (to do something)
llenar	to fill
lleno	full
llevar	to carry
llevar (al hospital)	to take (to hospital)
llevar (ropa)	to wear (clothes)
llevo un año aquí	I have been here a year
llorar	to cry (tears)
llover	to rain
llover a cántaros	to pour with rain
la **llovizna**	drizzle
la **lluvia**	rain

la **maceta**	flowerpot
la **madera**	wood (material)
la **madre**	mother
¡**Madre** mía!	Gosh!
la **madrugada**	early morning
madrugar	to get up early
el **maestro**/la **maestra**	teacher
el **magnetofón**	cassette recorder
mal	badly
la **maleta**	suitcase
malo	bad
mamá	Mummy
La **Mancha**	The English Channel
la **mancha**	stain
mandar	to send *enviar*
la **manera**	way (of doing something)
la **manga**	sleeve
la **manifestación**	demonstration
la **mano**	hand
la **manta**	blanket
el **mantel**	tablecloth
mantener	to maintain
la **mantequilla**	butter
la **manzana**	apple
el **manzano**	apple tree
mañana	tomorrow
mañana por la **mañana**	tomorrow morning
pasado **mañana**	the day after tomorrow
por la **mañana**	in the morning
el **maquillaje**	make-up
la **máquina**	machine
la **máquina** de escribir	typewriter

la **máquina** fotográfica	camera
el/la **mar**	sea
la **marca**	make (e.g. of car)
marcar un gol	to score a goal
marcar un número	to dial a number
marcharse	to go away
la **marea**	tide
mareado	feeling ill
marearse	to feel sick
el **mareo**	nausea
el **marido**	husband
el **marinero**	sailor
los **mariscos**	shellfish
marrón	brown
más	more
más bien	rather
el **matador**	bullfighter
matar	to kill
la **matrícula**	registration (of a car)
el **matrimonio**	married couple
la **mayonesa**	mayonnaise
mayor	bigger
la **mayoría**	majority
el **mayúsculo**	capital letter
máximo	maximum
la **mecanógrafa**	typist
la **mecanografía**	typing
el **mechero**	cigarette lighter
la **media**	stocking
a **mediados** de	about the middle o
mediano	medium
la **medianoche**	midnight
el **médico**	doctor
medio	half
el **mediodía**	midday

medir	to measure
el mejillón	mussel
mejor	better
mejorar	to improve
el melocotón	peach
menor	smaller
menos	less
¡Menos mal!	Thank goodness!
mensual	monthly
la mentira	lie
mentiroso	untruthful
el menú del día	menu of the day
el menú turístico	menu for tourists
a menudo	often
el mercado	market
merecer	to deserve
merendar	to picnic; to have tea
la merienda	picnic; afternoon tea
la merluza	hake
la mermelada	marmalade
el mes	month
la mesa	table
la mesilla de noche	bedside table
meter	to put [in], insert
el metro	metre
el miedo	fear
la película de miedo	horror film
el miembro	member
mientras	while
la mina	mine
el minero	miner
mínimo	minimum
la minoría	minority
la minúscula	small letter

mirar	to look at
la **misa**	mass (religious service)
el colegio	
mismo	the school itself
el **mismo** colegio	the same school
la **mitad**	half
la **mochila**	rucksack
la **moda**	fashion
el **modo**	the way (of doing something)
mojado	soaked
mojado hasta los huesos	soaked to the skin
mojarse	to get soaked
molestar	to bother
la **moneda**	coin
la **moneda** extranjera	foreign currency
el **mono**	monkey
la **montaña**	mountain
montañoso	mountainous
montar a caballo	to ride (horses)
el **monte**	mountain
morder	to bite
moreno	dark (complexion)
morir 29	to die
la **mosca**	fly (i.e. insect)
la **mostaza**	mustard
el **mostrador**	counter (in shop)
mostrar	to show
la **moto**	motorbike
mover	to move
el **mozo**	porter; waiter
el **muchacho**/la **muchacha**	boy/girl
la **muchedumbre**	crowd

la **mudanza**	change; move (of house)
mudarse	*change clothes* to move house
mudo	mute
los **muebles**	furniture
la **muela**	tooth (a molar)
muerto	dead
la **mujer**	woman
la **multa**	fine (i.e. money)
el **mundo**	world
todo el **mundo**	everybody
la **muñeca**	wrist
la **muñeca** de niño	doll
la **muralla**	wall (e.g. round a town)
el **muro**	wall (outside)
el **museo**	museum
la **música** pop	pop music
la **música** rock	rock music
el **músico**	musician
muy	very

_____ _____
_____ _____
_____ _____
_____ _____

nacer	to be born
nacido	born
el **nacimiento**	birth
la **nación**	nation
nada	nothing
¡de **nada**!	don't mention it!

nadar	to swim
nadie	nobody
los **naipes**	playing cards
la **naranja**	orange (the fruit)
la **naranjada**	orangeade
la **nariz**	nose
la **nata**	cream
la **natación**	swimming
natural	native (of a country)
la **Navidad**	Christmas
la **neblina**	fog
necesitar	to need
necio	silly
negarse a	to refuse
el hombre de	
negocios	businessman
negro	black
el **neumático**	tyre
nevar	to snow
la **nevera**	fridge
¡**ni** hablar!	unthinkable!
ni … **ni** …	neither … nor
la **niebla**	fog
el **nieto**/la **nieta**	grandson/daughter
la **nieve**	snow
ninguno	no
el **niño**/la **niña**	boy/girl
el **nivel**	level
la **noche**	night
la **Nochebuena**	Christmas Eve
la **Nochevieja**	New Year's Eve
el **nombre**	name
el **norte**	the north
la **nota**	mark (e.g. in an exam)

las **noticias**	the news
el **novio**/la **novia**	boyfriend/girlfriend
la **nube**	cloud
nublado	cloudy
la **nubosidad**	cloudiness
nuestro	our
nuevo	new
el **número** de teléfono	telephone number
nunca	never

---

o - o

silla o

o/u	or
obedecer	to obey
el **obispo**	bishop
el **objeto**	object
obligatorio	compulsory
la **obra**	work
la **obra** de teatro	play (at theatre)
obras (f)	works (e.g. roadworks)
el **obrero**	worker
no **obstante**	however
obtener	to obtain
ocupado	busy
ocurrir 5	to happen
odiar	to hate
el **oeste**	the west

ocuparse de

la película del oeste	western (film)
la oferta	offer
el oficial	official
la oficina de objetos perdidos	lost-property office
la oficina de turismo	tourist office
ofrecer	to offer
¡oiga!	Listen!
oír 45	to hear
el ojo	eye
la ola	wave (sea)
oler	to smell
el olor	smell
olvidar	to forget
opinar	to think (hold an opinion)
la oportunidad	opportunity
el ordenador	computer
la oreja	ear
orgulloso	proud
el origen	origin
la orilla	bank (of river)
a orillas del mar	at the seaside
el oro	gold
la orquesta	orchestra
la oscuridad	darkness
oscuro = obscuro	dark
el oso	bear (the animal)
el otoño	autumn
otro	other
la oveja	sheep

el **padre**	father
los **padres**	parents
pagar	to pay
la **página**	page
el **pago**	payment
el **país**	country
el **paisaje**	countryside
la **paja**	straw
el **pájaro**	bird
la **pala**	spade
la **palabra**	word
pálido	pale
el **palillo**	toothpick
la **paloma**	dove
el **pan**	bread
la **panadería**	bakery
el **panadero**	baker
el **panecillo**	roll (bread)
los **pantalones**	pair of trousers
la **pantalla**	screen
el **pañuelo**	handkerchief
papá (*m*)	daddy
el **papel**	paper
el **papel** higiénico	toilet paper
la **papelería**	stationer
el **par**	pair
para	for
el **parabrisas**	windscreen
la **parada** de autobuses	bus stop
el **parado**	unemployed person
el **parador**	hotel (government-run)
el **paraguas**	umbrella
parar	to stop
el **parasol**	sunshade
parecer	to seem

parecerse a	to resemble
parecido	similar
la pared	wall (inside)
la pareja	couple
los parientes	relatives
el paro	unemployment
el parque de atracciones	amusement park
por todas partes	everywhere
particular	private
el partido	match (e.g. footbal|)
partir	to depart
a partir de	from
el pasado	the past
el lunes pasado	last Monday
pasado mañana	the day after tomorrow
el pasajero	passenger
pasar	to spend (time)
pasar	to happen
pasar lista	to call the register
pasarlo bien (mal)	to have a good (ba| time
el pasatiempo	pastime
la Pascua de Navidad	Christmas
la Pascua de Resurrección	Easter
pasearse	to go for a walk
el paseo	stroll
dar un paseo	to go for a stroll
dar un paseo en barco de vela	to go for a sail
el pasillo	corridor
el paso	step
el paso a nivel	level crossing
el paso de peatones	pedestrian crossin|
la pasta de dientes	toothpaste
el pastel	cake
la pastelería	cake shop

la **pastilla**	tablet
patatas fritas (*f*)	chips
el **patín**	skate
el **patinaje**	skating
patinar	to skate
el **patio**	yard (paved area)
el **pato**	duck
el **patrón**	boss
la **patrulla**	patrol
el **pavo**	turkey
el **payaso**	clown
la **paz**	peace
el **peaje**	toll (on motorway)
el **peatón**	pedestrian
el **pecho**	chest (part of your body)
el **pedazo**	piece
pedir	to ask for
pedir prestado	to borrow
pegar	to hit
peinarse	to comb your hair
el **peine**	comb
la **pelea**	fight
pelear	to fight
la **película**	film (e.g. at cinema)
el **peligro**	danger
peligroso	dangerous
pelirrojo	red-haired
el **pelo**	hair
la **pelota**	ball (e.g. a football)
la **peluquería**	hairdresser's (place)
el **peluquero**	hairdresser (person)
valer la **pena**	to be worthwhile
el **pendiente**	earring
la **pendiente**	slope
pensar	to think

la **pensión**	boarding-house
pensión completa (*f*)	full board
media **pensión**	half board
peor	worse
pequeño	small
la **pera**	pear
el **peral**	pear tree
perder	to lose
la **pérdida**	loss
¡**perdón**!	excuse me!
perdonar	to excuse
perezoso	lazy
el **periódico**	newspaper
el **periodista**	journalist
la **perla**	pearl
permanecer	to stay
el **permiso** de conducir	driving licence
permitir	to allow
pero	but
el **perro**	dog
perseguir	to pursue
la **persiana**	blind (on a window)
pertenecer	to belong
pesado	heavy
pesar	to weigh
a **pesar** de	in spite of
la **pescadería**	fishmonger's
el **pescadero**	fishmonger
el **pescado**	fish (when dead)
el **pescador**	fisherman
el **peso**	weight
el **pez**	fish (when alive)
la **picadura**	bite (e.g. insect)
picar	to bite (e.g. insects)
a la una y **pico**	a little after one o'clock

el **pie**	foot
la **piedra**	stone
la **piel**	skin
la **pierna**	leg
el **pijama**	pyjamas
la **pila**	battery (e.g. for torch)
el nombre de **pila**	first name
la **pimienta**	pepper (white)
el **pimiento**	pepper (e.g. red)
el **pinchazo**	puncture
el **ping-pong**	table tennis
pintar	to paint
el **pintor**	painter
la **pintura**	painting
la **piña**	pineapple
la **pipa**	a pipe
los **Pireneos**	the Pyrenees
pisar	to tread on
la **piscina**	swimming pool
el **piso**	flat (i.e. apartment)
el segundo **piso**	the second floor
la **pista** de patinaje	skating rink
el **pito**	whistle
la **pizarra**	blackboard
planchar	to iron
el **plano**	map (e.g. of a city)
la **planta**	plant
la **planta** baja	ground floor
la **plata**	silver
el **plátano**	banana
el **platillo**	saucer
el **plato**	plate
el **plato** principal	main course

(handwritten annotation: "race track" next to la pista de patinaje)

la **playa**	beach
la **plaza**	square (in a town)
la **plaza** de toros	bullring
la silla **plegable**	folding chair
el **plomo**	lead (metal)
la **población**	population
pobre	poor
la **pobreza**	poverty
poco	little (not much)
pocos	few
poder	to be able
la **policía**	police
el **policía**	policeman
el **polvo**	dust
el **pollo**	chicken
poner	to put
poner la mesa	to lay the table
ponerse	to become
ponerse un abrigo	to put a coat on
ponerse a trabajar	to begin to (work)
por casualidad	by chance
por ciento	per cent
por ejemplo	for example
por favor	please
por lo menos	at least
por lo tanto	therefore
¿**por** qué?	why?
porque	because
el **portero**	caretaker
portugués/Portugal (*m*)	Portuguese/ Portugal
el **porvenir**	the future
poseer	to possess
la **postal**	postcard
el **postre**	dessert
potable	drinkable

practicar	to practise
el prado	meadow
el precio	price
precioso	wonderful *precious*
preciso	necessary; precise
preferir 27	to prefer
la pregunta	question
preguntar	to ask
preguntarse	to wonder
el premio	prize
la prensa	the press
preocupado	worried
preocuparse (de)	to worry
presentar	to introduce
prestar	to lend
la primavera	spring (season)
primero	first
el primo/la prima	cousin
la puerta	
principal	main door
el principio	beginning
la prisa	speed
el probador	fitting room
probarse	to try on
procedente de	coming from
procurar	to try
el profesor	teacher
profundo	deep
prohibido el paso	no entry
prometer	to promise
el pronóstico del tiempo	weather forecast
pronto	soon
mi propia casa	my own house
el propietario	owner
la propina	tip (money)
proponer	to suggest

proteger	to protect
próximo	next
el proyecto	plan
la prueba	test
la publicidad	advertising
el público	audience
el pueblo	town
el puente	bridge
la puerta	door
el puerto	port
pues	then
puesto que	since (because)
el pulpo	octopus
la pulsera	bracelet
hacer punto	to knit
a punto de	on the point of
a la una en punto	at one o'clock on the dot
el puro	cigar

¿qué?	what?
¡Qué horror!	How horrible!
¿Qué tal?	How are you?
quedar	to stay
¡Quédese con la vuelta!	Keep the change!
los quehaceres	chores (e.g. household)

quejarse	to complain
la **quemadura**	burn
quemar	to burn
querer	to want
querer decir	to mean
querido	dear (starting a letter)
el **queso**	cheese
quien	who
la **química**	chemistry
quince dias	fortnight
quinto	fifth
el **quiosco**	kiosk
quitar la mesa	to clear the table
quitar(se)	to take off (clothes)
quizá(s)	perhaps

_____ _____
_____ _____
_____ _____

la **ración**	portion
rápido	fast
el **rápido**	express train
raro	strange
la **rata**	rat
el **ratero**	pickpocket
el **rato**	short while
el **ratón**	mouse
los **ratos** libres	free time
la **razón**	reason

tener **razón**	to be right
realizar 73	to carry out
la **rebaja**	reduction
el **recado**	message
el/la **recepcionista**	receptionist
la **receta**	recipe
recibir 5	to receive
el **recibo**	receipt
reciente(mente)	recent(ly)
recomendar	to recommend
la **recompensa**	reward
reconocer	to recognize
recordar	to remember
el **recreo**	break-time (at school)
todo **recto**	straight on
el **recuerdo**	memory
la **red**	net
redondo	round
el **refresco**	refreshment (soft drink)
regalar	to give a present
el **regalo**	present (e.g. for birthday)
regar	to water
registrar	to search
la **regla**	rule(r)
regresar	to return
la **reina**	queen
el **Reino Unido**	United Kingdom
reír 10	to laugh
el **relámpago**	lightning
la **religión**	religion
el **reloj**	watch
la **relojería**	watchmaker's
rellenar	to fill

remar	to row (a boat)
el remedio	remedy
RENFE	Spanish Railways
la reparación	repair
reparar	to repair
repasar	to revise (for exams)
de repente	suddenly
el/la representante	representative
la rueda de repuesto	spare wheel
resbalar	to slip
rescatar	to rescue
el rescate	rescue
el resfriado	cold (i.e. the illness)
respirar	to breathe
responder	to answer
la respuesta	reply
el retraso	delay
el retrete	toilet
la reunión	meeting
reunirse	to come together
el revisor	guard (on train)
la revista	magazine
el rey	king
rico	rich
el riesgo	risk
el rincón	corner (inside)
el río	river
la risa	laughter
robar	to steal
la rodilla	knee
rogar	to ask
rojo	red
romper	to break
el ron	rum
la ropa	clothes

el vino **rosado**	rosé wine
el **rostro**	face
rubio	blond
la **rueda**	wheel
el **ruido**	noise
ruidoso	noisy
ruso/Rusia (*f*)	Russian/Russia
la **rutina**	routine

_____   _____

_____   _____

_____   _____

la **sábana**	sheet (on bed)
saber	to know (somethin
el **sabor**	flavour
el **sacacorchos**	corkscrew
sacar	to take out (i.e. extract)
el **sacerdote**	a priest
el **saco** de dormir	sleeping bag
la **sal**	salt
la **sala** de espera	waiting-room
la **sala** de estar	living-room
la **salchicha**	sausage
el **salchichón**	sausage (large) (salami)
la **salida**	exit
salir 42	to go out
el **salón**	lounge
la **salsa**	sauce
saltar	to jump

la **salud**	health
¡**salud**!	cheers!
saludar	to greet
los **saludos**	greetings
salvaje	wild
salvar	to save (e.g. from danger)
la **sandalia**	sandal
la **sangre**	blood
sano y salvo	safe and sound
el **santo**/la **santa**	saint
la **sartén**	frying-pan
el **sastre**	tailor
satisfacer	to satisfy
el **secador**	hair-dryer
secar	to dry
seco	dry
secuestrar	to kidnap
el **secuestro**	kidnapping
la **sed**	thirst
la **seda**	silk
todo **seguido**	straight on
seguir 68	to follow
según	according to
el **segundo**	second (of time)
seguro	sure
el **seguro**	insurance
el **sello**	stamp
los **semáforos**	traffic lights
la **semana**	week
la **Semana** Santa	Holy Week
semejante	similar
sencillo	simple
el **sendero** = la senda	path
sentarse	to sit down
sentir(se) 27	to feel

la	**señal**	sign
las	**señas**	address
	séptimo	seventh
	serio	serious
los	**servicios**	toilets
la	**servilleta**	serviette
la	**sesión**	performance (at cinema)
el	**seto**	hedge
	severo	strict
	sexto	sixth
	si	if
	sí	yes
la	**sidra**	cider
	siempre	always
la	**sierra**	range of mountains
el	**siglo**	century
	significar	to mean
	siguiente	following
	silbar	to whistle
	silencioso	silent
la	**silla**	chair
el	**sillón**	armchair
	simpático	nice (of people)
	sin	without
	sin embargo	however
el	**sindicato**	trades union
	sino	but (after a negative)
el	**síntoma**	symptom
el	**sitio**	place
¿hay	**sitio?**	Is there any room?
	situado	situated
	sobre	on
	sobresaliente	outstanding
el	**sobrino**/la **sobrina**	nephew/niece

Ser

Servir

¡Socorro!	Help!
el sol	sun
solamente	only
el soldado	soldier
soler	to usually do something
solitario	lonely
solo *adj*	alone
sólo *adv*	only
el soltero/la soltera	bachelor/spinster
la sombra	shadow
el sombrero	hat
sonar	to sound
sonreír	to smile
la sonrisa	smile
soñar	to dream
la sopa	soup
soplar	to blow
sordo	deaf
la sorpresa	surprise
el sorteo	draw (in a lottery)
la sortija	ring (on a finger)
sospechoso	suspicious
el sótano	basement
suave	soft
la subida	climb
subir 5	to go up
súbito	sudden
el suburbio	suburb
suceder	to happen
el suceso	event
sucio	dirty
sudar	to sweat
el suegro/la suegra	father/mother-in-law
el sueldo	salary

el **suelo**	floor (of a room)
el **sueño**	dream
la **suerte**	luck
sufrir	to suffer
suizo/Suiza (f)	Swiss/Switzerland
el **súper**	petrol (high-grade)
el **supermercado**	supermarket
suponer	to suppose
el **sur**	the south
el **surtidor**	fountain
suspender	to fail (someone in an exam)
sustituir	to substitute
el **susto**	fright

_____ _____
_____ _____
_____ _____

_____

la **tabacalera**	tobacconist (shop)
la **taberna**	tavern
el **taburete**	stool
el **tacón**	heel
¿Qué **tal?**	How are you?
tal persona	such a person
tal vez	perhaps
TALGO	train (special service)
la **talla**	size (of a person)
el **taller**	workshop
el **tamaño**	size

también	also
tampoco	neither
tan (contento)	so (happy)
tanto	so much
tanto ... como	as much ... as
la **tapa**	bar snack
la **tapia**	wall
la **taquigrafía**	shorthand
la **taquilla**	ticket office
el **taquillero**	ticket clerk
tardar	to take time (to do)
la **tarde**	evening
tarde	late
la **tarea**	task
la **tarifa**	price list
la **tarjeta**	card
la **tarjeta** de crédito	credit card
la **tarta**	tart
el **taxista**	taxi driver
la **taza**	cup
el **té**	tea
el **teatro**	theatre
el **tebeo**	comic (child's magazine)
el **techo**	ceiling
el **tejado**	roof
la **tela**	cloth
telefonear	to telephone
el **televisor**	television set
temblar	to tremble
la **tempestad**	storm
temprano	early
el **tendero**	shopkeeper
tenderse	to lie down
el **tenedor**	fork
tener	to have

tener calor	to be hot (people)
tener éxito	to be successful
tener frío	to be cold (people)
tener ganas de *feel like*	to want to
tener hambre	to be hungry
tener lugar	to take place
tener miedo	to be afraid
tener prisa	to be in a hurry
tener que	to have to
tener razón	to be right
tener sed	to be thirsty
tener sueño	to be sleepy
tener suerte	to be lucky
tercero	third
terminar	to finish
el termómetro	thermometer
la ternera	veal
la terraza	the area outside a café
el terremoto	earthquake
el terreno de camping	camp site
el testigo	witness
la tetera	teapot
tibio	lukewarm
el tiempo	weather
pasar tiempo	to spend time
la tienda	shop
la tienda (de campaña)	tent
la tierra	ground; earth
el tigre	tiger
las tijeras	scissors
el timbre	bell (small)
tímido	shy
las tinieblas	darkness
el vino tinto	red wine
el tío/la tía	uncle/aunt

el tipo	type
típico	typical
tirar	to pull *to throw*
tiritar	to shiver
el título	title
la tiza	chalk
la toalla	towel
el tobillo	ankle
el tocadiscos	record-player
el tocador	dressing-table
tocar	to touch
tocar la guitarra	to play the guitar
todavía	still
todo	all
tolerar	to tolerate
tomar	to take
tonto	stupid
torcer	to turn (e.g. to right)
torear	to fight bulls
el torero	bullfighter
la tormenta	storm
el toro	bull
torpe	clumsy
la torre	tower
la tortilla	omelette
la tortuga	turtle
la tos	cough
toser	to cough
el pan tostado	toast
trabajador	hard-working
trabajar	to work
el trabajo	work
traducir	to translate
traer	to bring
tragar	to swallow
el traje	suit (clothes)

el **traje de baño**	swimming costume
tranquilo	calm
el **transbordo**	change (of trains)
el **transeúnte**	passer-by
el **tranvía**	tram
trasladar	to move
el **tratamiento**	treatment
tratar	to try
a **través de**	across
travieso	naughty
el **tren**	train
el **trimestre**	term (e.g. at school)
triste	sad
tronar	to thunder
el **trozo**	piece
la **trucha**	trout
el **trueno**	thunder
tumbarse	to lie down
una oficina de **turismo**	tourist office
el menú **turístico**	tourist menu
el **turrón**	sweet (made from almonds)
tutear	to use 'tú'

tramo   lap span stair flight passage

último	last (of series)
único	only
unos, unas	some
usar	to use
útil	useful
utilizar	to use
la uva	grape

la vaca	cow
las vacaciones	holidays
vacilar	to hesitate
vacío	empty
¿Vale?	Okay?
vale la pena	it is worth while
valer	to be worth
valiente	brave
el valle	valley
varios	several
el vaso	glass
a veces	sometimes
la vecindad	neighbourhood
el/la vecino/-a	neighbour
la vela	sail
la velocidad	speed
la venda	bandage
vendar	to bandage
el vendedor	seller (of goods)

vender	to sell
venir	to come
la venta	sale
la ventana	window
la ventanilla	window (small)
ver	to see
veranear	to spend the summer
el verano	summer
de veras	truly
la verdad	truth
verdadero	true
verde	green
la verdura	vegetable
ver	to see
el vestíbulo	hall (in a house)
el vestido	dress
vestirse	to dress
el vestuario	dressing-room
la vez	time (occasion)
de vez en cuando	from time to time
la vía	track (railway)
viajar	to travel
el viaje	journey
el viajero	traveller
la vida	life
el vidrio	glass (material)
viejo	old
el viento	wind
el vientre	belly
el villancico	carol
el vinagre	vinegar
el vino	wine
el violín	violin
visitar	to visit
la víspera	the day before
la vista	view

el **viudo**/la **viuda**	widower/widow
la **vivienda**	dwelling
vivir 5	to live
vivo	alive, bright, vivid
el **volante**	steering wheel
volar	to fly
volver	to return
volverse	to turn around
la **voz**	voice
el **vuelo**	flight
dar una **vuelta** TO TURN AROUND	to go for a stroll
la **vuelta**	change (e.g. money); return

_____   _____
_____   _____
_____   _____

ABCDEFGHIJKLMNOPQRSTUV**W**XYZ

el **wáter**	toilet

_____   _____
_____   _____
_____   _____

ABCDEFGHIJKLMNOPQRSTUVWX**Y**Z

ya	now
ya que	since (because)
el **yogur**	yogurt

zambullirse 9	to dive
la **zanahoria**	carrot
la **zapatería**	shoe shop
el **zapatero**	shoemaker
la **zapatilla**	slipper
el **zapato**	shoe
el **zumo**	juice

_____   _____
_____   _____
_____   _____
_____   _____
_____   _____

398 verbs

$5 \times 7 \times 7 \times 10$

35×70

$7 \times 7 \times 50$

$49 \times 50 = 2450$

ENGLISH-SPANISH

about (approximately)	más o menos
about (concerning)	acerca de
above	encima
abroad	el extranjero
absent	ausente
to be **absent**	faltar
absolutely	absolutamente
Absolutely not!	¡En absoluto!
accent	el acento
to **accept**	aceptar
acceptable	aceptable
accident	el accidente
to **accompany**	acompañar
according to	según
accurate	exacto
accustomed	acostumbrado
to **acquire**	adquerir
across	a través de
action	la acción
activity	la actividad
actor/actress	el actor/la actriz
to **add**	añadir
in **addition** to	además de
address	las señas; la dirección
to **admit**	admitir
adult	el adulto
advanced	adelantado
adventure	la aventura
advertisement	el anuncio
advertising	la publicidad
to **advise**	aconsejar
affection	el cariño
affectionate	cariñoso
after	después
against	contra

age	la edad
agitated	agitado
two years ago	hace dos años
agreed	de acuerdo
agreement	el acuerdo
agriculture	la agricultura
air	el aire
air-conditioning	el aire acondicionado
air hostess	la azafata
airport	el aeropuerto
alarm clock	el despertador
alarm signal	la señal de alarma
album	el álbum
alive	vivo
all	todo
to allow	permitir
allowed	autorizado
almost	casi
alone	solo
along	a lo largo de
also	también
although	aunque
always	siempre
ambition	la ambición
ambitious	ambicioso
ambulance	la ambulancia
American	americano
amusement park	el parque de atracciones
anchovy	el boquerón
ancient	antiguo
to get angry	enfadarse
animal	el animal
ankle	el tobillo

to **announce**	anunciar
to **annoy**	fastidiar
annoyed	enojado
answer	la contestación
to **answer**	contestar; responder
apartment	el apartamento
aperitif	el aperitivo
to **appear**	aparecer
appetite	el apetito
apple	la manzana
apple tree	el manzano
appointment	la cita
to **appreciate**	apreciar
apprentice	el aprendiz
to **approach**	acercarse; aproximarse
approximately	aproximadamente
apricot	el albaricoque
architect	el arquitecto
architecture	la arquitectura
the **area** around	los alrededores
the **area** outside a cafe	la terraza
Argentinian/Argentina	argentino/ Argentina (f)
arm (of body)	el brazo
armchair	la butaca; el sillón
around	alrededor de
arrival	la llegada
to **arrive**	llegar
art	el arte
artichoke	la alcachofa
article	el artículo
artist	el/la artista
as	como
as much … as	tanto …… como
to **ask**	preguntar; rogar

to ask for	pedir
asparagus	los espárragos
aspirin	la aspirina
astonished	atónito
at least	por lo menos
athletics	el atletismo
atmosphere	el ambiente
to attack	atacar
attack	el ataque
attention	la atención
attractive	atractivo
audience	el público
aunt	la tía
Austrian/Austria	austriaco/Austria (
author/ess	el autor/la autora
automatic	automático
autumn	el otoño
avenue	la avenida
avocado	el aguacate
to avoid	evitar

_____   _____
_____   _____
_____   _____
_____   _____
_____   _____

ABCDEFGHIJKLMNOPQRSTUVWXY

baby	el bebé
bachelor	el soltero
back (of your body)	la espalda
bad	malo
badly	mal

bag	la bolsa
baker	el panadero
bakery	la panadería
balcony	el balcón
balcony (in cinema)	el anfiteatro
bald	calvo
ball (e.g. a football)	la pelota
ballpoint	el bolígrafo
banana	el plátano
bandage	la venda
to bandage	vendar
bank (in High Street)	el banco
bank (of river)	la orilla
banknote	el billete de banco
bar (for refreshment)	el bar
bar snack	la tapa
bargain sale	la liquidación
basement	el sótano
basket	el cesto/la cesta
basketball	el baloncesto
bath	el baño
to bathe	bañarse
bathing costume	el traje de baño
battery (in a car)	la batería
battery (e.g. for torch)	la pila
bay	la bahía
to be	estar; ser
to be able	poder
to be afraid	tener miedo
to be cold (people)	tener frío
to be enough	bastar
to be frightened	asustarse
to be happy	alegrarse
to be hot (people)	tener calor
to be hungry	tener hambre
to be in a hurry	tener prisa

to be interested in	interesarse en
to be lucky	tener suerte
to be present at	asistir
to be right	tener razón
to be sleepy	tener sueño
to be successful	tener éxito
to be thirsty	tener sed
to be worth	valer
beach	la playa
bean	la haba; la judía
bear	el oso
beard	la barba
beautiful	bello; hermoso
because	porque
because of	a causa de
to become	ponerse
bed	la cama
bedroom	el dormitorio
bedside table	la mesilla de noche
bee	la abeja
I have been here a year	llevo un año aquí
beer	la cerveza
before	antes
to begin to	comenzar a; empezar a; ponerse a
the beginning	el principio
behind	atrás; detrás de
Belgian/Belgium	belga/Bélgica (f)
to believe	creer
bell (e.g. on a church)	la campana
bell (small)	el timbre
belly	el vientre
to belong	pertenecer
below	bajo
belt	el cinturón

bench	el banco
beret	la boina
beside	al lado de
besides	además
better	mejor
between	entre
bicycle	la bicicleta
big	grande
big shops	los grandes almacenes
bigger	mayor
bikini	el bikini
bill (in a cafe)	la cuenta
billiards	el billar
biology	la biología
bird	el pájaro
birth	el nacimiento
birthday	el cumpleaños
biscuit	el bizcocho; la galleta
bishop	el obispo
to bite	morder
to bite (e.g. insects)	picar
bite (e.g. insect)	la picadura
bitter	amargo
black	negro
blackboard	la pizarra
blame	la culpa
blanket	la manta
Bless you (on sneezing)	¡Jesús!
blind	ciego
blind (on window)	la persiana
blond	rubio
blood	la sangre
blouse	la blusa
blow	el golpe

to **blow**	soplar
blue	azul
on **board**	a bordo
boarding-house	la pensión
boat	el barco
body	el cuerpo
to **boil**	hervir
bone	el hueso
book	el libro
bookshop	la librería
boot	la bota
border	la frontera
to be **bored**	aburrirse
bored, boring	aburrido
to be **born**	nacer
born	nacido
to **borrow**	pedir prestado
boss	el amo; el patrón
both	ambos
to **bother**	molestar
bottle	la botella
bottle-opener	el abrebotellas
box	la caja
box (large)	el cajón
boy	el chico; el muchacho; el niñ
boyfriend	el novio
bracelet	la pulsera
to **brake**	frenar
brakes	los frenos
brandy	el aguardiente
brave	valiente
bread	el pan
to **break**	romper
to **break** down (mechanical)	averiarse
break-time (at school)	el recreo

breakdown (mechanical)	la avería
to breakfast	desayunar
breakfast	el desayuno
to breathe	respirar
breeze	la brisa
bricklayer	el albañil
bridge	el puente
briefcase	la cartera
to bring	traer
British	británico
brochure	el folleto
broken down (mechanical)	averiado
brooch	el broche
brother	el hermano
brother-in-law	el cuñado
brown	marrón; castaño
brush (toothbrush)	el cepillo (de dientes)
bucket	el cubo
to build	construir
building	el edificio
bulb (light)	la bombilla
bull	el toro
bullfight	la corrida de toros
bullfighter	el torero; el matador
bullring	la plaza de toros
burn	la quemadura
to burn	arder; quemar
bus	el autobús
bus-station	la estación de autobuses
bus-stop	la parada de autobuses
businessman	el hombre de negocios
busy	ocupado
but	pero

but (after a negative)	sino
butcher	el carnicero
butcher's (shop)	la carnicería
butter	la mantequilla
button	el botón
to buy	comprar
by chance	por casualidad

_____ _____
_____ _____
_____ _____
_____ _____

_____

café	la cafetería
cage	la jaula
cake	el pastel
cake shop	la pastelería
to calculate	calcular
call	la llamada
to call	llamar
to call the register	pasar lista
to be called	llamarse
calm	tranquilo
camera	la cámara; la máquina fotográfica
to camp	acampar; hacer camping
camp site	el terreno de camping
canal	el canal

candle	la bujía
canteen	la cantina
cap	la gorra
capable	capaz
the capital (city)	la capital
capital letter	el mayúsculo
captain	el capitán
car	el coche
caramel custard	el flan
caravan	la caravana
card	la tarjeta
playing cards	los naipes, las cartas
care	el cuidado
career	la carrera
caretaker	el portero
carol	el villancico
car park	el aparcamiento
carpenter	el carpintero
carpet	la alfombra
carrot	la zanahoria
to carry	llevar
to carry out	realizar
cartoons	los dibujos animados
cashier	el cajero
cassette recorder	el magnetofón
castanets	las castañuelas
castle	el castillo
cat	el gato
cathedral	la catedral
cauliflower	la coliflor
ceiling	el techo
cellar	la bodega
centre	el centro
century	el siglo

chain	la cadena
chair	la silla
chalk	la tiza
champion	el campeón
championship	el campeonato
to change	cambiar
change	el cambio; la mudanza
change (of trains)	el transbordo
change (e.g. money)	la vuelta
the (English) Channel	La Mancha
channel (on TV)	la cadena
to charge (a battery)	cargar (una batería)
to chat	charlar
cheap	barato
to check	comprobar
to check (passports)	controlar
checkout	la caja (in supermarket)
Cheer up!	¡Ánimo!
Cheers!	¡Salud!
cheese	el queso
chemist (shop)	la farmacia
chemistry	la química
cherry	la cereza
chess	el ajedrez
chest (part of your body)	el pecho
chicken	el pollo
chicken in garlic	el pollo al ajillo
chief	el jefe
childlike	infantil
chimney	la chimenea
chips	patatas fritas (f)
chocolate	el chocolate
to choose	elegir; escoger

chop (of meat)	la chuleta
chores (e.g. household)	los quehaceres
Christmas	la Navidad
Christmas Eve	la Nochebuena
church	la iglesia
cider	la sidra
cigar	el cigarro; el puro
cigarette	el cigarillo
cigarette lighter	el mechero
cinema	el cine
circus	el circo
citizen	el ciudadano
city	la ciudad
the Civil Guard	la Guardia Civil
clam	la almeja
classic	clásico
classroom	la aula
to clean	limpiar
clean	limpio
clever	hábil
to be clever	ser listo
cliff	el acantilado
climate	el clima
climb	la subida
climber	el/la alpinista
climbing	el alpinismo
to close	cerrar
closed	cerrado
cloth	la tela
clothes	la ropa
cloud	la nube
cloudiness	la nubosidad
cloudy	anublado; nublado
clown	el payaso
club	el club
clumsy	torpe

coach (vehicle)	el autocar
coast	la costa
coat	el abrigo
cod	el bacalao
coffee (white)	el cafe con leche
coffee (with some milk)	el cafe cortado
coffee (black)	el cafe solo
coffee-pot	la cafetera
coin	la moneda
cold	frío
cold (the illness)	el resfriado
having a	
cold	constipado
to **collect**	coleccionar
collection	la colección
to **collide** with	chocar con
colour	el color
comb	el peine
to **comb** your hair	peinarse
to **come**	venir
to **come** together	reunirse
comfortable	cómodo
comic (child's magazine)	el tebeo
coming from	procedente de
to **commit**	cometer
company	la compañía
compartment (on train)	el departamento
competition	el concurso
to **complain**	quejarse
compulsory	obligatorio
computer	el computador; el ordenador
concert	el concierto
conference	conferencia
Congratulations!	¡Enhorabuena!

to **contain**	contener
to **continue**	continuar
to **control**	controlar
to **cook**	cocinar
cook (the person)	el cocinero
to be **cool** weather	hacer fresco
to **copy**	copiar
corkscrew	el sacacorchos
corner (outside)	la esquina
corner (inside)	el rincón
to **correct**	corregir
correct	justo
corridor	el pasillo
to **cost**	costar
cotton	el algodón
cough	la tos
to **cough**	toser
counter (in shop)	el mostrador
country	el país
countryside	el campo; el paisaje
couple	la pareja
course	el curso
cousin	el primo/la prima
cow	la vaca
coward	el cobarde
crane	la grúa
cream	la crema; la nata
to **create**	crear
credit card	la tarjeta de crédito
cricket	el criquet
crime	el crimen
to **cross**	atravesar; cruzar
crossroads	el cruce
crowd	la muchedumbre
to **cry** (tears)	llorar

cup	la taza
foreign **currency**	la moneda extranjera
curtain	la cortina
cushion	el cojín
custom	la costumbre
customer	el/la cliente
customs (-office)	la aduana
customs duties	los derechos de aduana
customs officer	el aduanero
to **cut**	cortar
cycling	el ciclismo
cyclist	el/la ciclista

Daddy	papá (*m*)
daily	diario
dairy	la lechería
damage	el daño
damp	húmedo
to **dance**	bailar
dance	el baile
danger	el peligro
dangerous	peligroso
to **dare**	atreverse
dark	oscuro
dark (complexion)	moreno
darkness	la oscuridad; las tinieblas
date (of the month)	la fecha
daughter	la hija
day	el día

the **day** after tomorrow	pasado mañana
the **day** before	la víspera
the **day** before yesterday	anteayer
dead	muerto
deaf	sordo
dear (expensive)	caro
dear (starting a letter)	querido
decayed	carcomido
to **decide**	decidir
to **declare**	declarar
deep	profundo
delay	el retraso
delayed	atrasado
to **delight**	encantar
to **deliver**	entregar
demonstration	la manifestación
dentist	el dentista
to **depart**	partir
descent	la bajada
to **describe**	describir
description	la descripción
to **deserve**	merecer
dessert	el postre
destination	el destino
to **destroy**	destrozar
detail	el detalle
detour	el desvío
to **dial** a number	marcar un número
diamond	el diamante
diarrhoea	la diarrea
diary	la agenda
dictionary	el diccionario
to **die**	morir
difference	la diferencia
different	diferente; distinto
difficult	difícil

difficulty	la dificultad
dining car (on a train)	el coche-comedor (restorán)
dining-room	el comedor
direction	la dirección
dirty	sucio
to **disappear**	desaparecer
disaster	el desastre
disco	la discoteca
to **discover**	descubrir
disgust	el asco
to **disgust**	dar asco
How **disgusting!**	¡Qué asco!
disgusting	asqueroso
dishwasher	el lavaplatos
to **disobey**	desobedecer
distance	la distancia
distant	lejano
district	el barrio
to **dive**	zambullirse
divorced	divorciado
to **do**	hacer
doctor	el doctor; el médico
document	el documento
dog	el perro
doll	la muñeca de niño
Don't mention it!	¡De nada!
donkey	el burro
door	la puerta
double	doble
double bed	la cama de matrimonio; la cama doble
double room	la habitación doble
doubt	la duda
dove	la paloma
downstairs	abajo

dozen	la docena
to draw	dibujar
draw (in a lottery)	el sorteo
drawer	el cajón
drawing	el dibujo
dream	el sueño
to dream	soñar
dress (lady's)	el vestido
to dress	vestirse
dressing-gown	la bata
dressing-table	el tocador
dressing-room	el vestuario
to drink	beber
drink	la bebida
drink (of liquor)	la copa
drink made from almonds	la horchata
drinkable	potable
to drive	conducir
driver	el/la automovilista; el conductor; el chófer
driving licence	el permiso de conducir; el carnet de conducir
drizzle	la llovizna
drop	la gota
to drown	ahogarse
drug	la droga
drunk	borracho
to dry	secar
dry	seco
duck	el pato
during	durante
dust	el polvo
dustman	el basurero
Dutch	holandés
dwelling	la vivienda

	each	cada
	ear	la oreja
	earring	el pendiente
	early	temprano
	early morning	la madrugada
to	earn your living	ganarse la vida
	earth	la tierra
	earthquake	el terremoto
the	east	el este
	Easter	la Pascua de Resurrección
	easy	fácil
to	eat	comer
to	eat (evening meal)	cenar
	education	la educación; la enseñanza
	effort	el esfuerzo
	egg	el huevo
	elbow	el codo
	electric cooker	la cocina eléctrica
	electricity	la electricidad
	elegant	elegante
	elephant	el elefante
	embassy	la embajada
to	embrace	abrazar
	embrace	el abrazo
	employee	el empleado
	empty	vacío
to	encourage	animar
	end	el fin
at the	end of	al cabo de
towards the		
	end of	a fines de
	engaged (phone)	¡está comunicado!
	engineer	el ingeniero
	English/England	inglés/Inglaterra (f

Enjoy your meal!	¡Qué aproveche!
to **enjoy** yourself	divertirse
enormous	enorme
enough	bastante; suficiente
to **enter**	entrar
enthusiast	el aficionado
entrance	la entrada
to **escape**	escaparse
Europe	Europa (*f*)
even	aun; incluso
evening	la tarde
the **evening** meal	la cena
event	el suceso
everybody	todo el mundo
everywhere	por todas partes
exactly	exactamente
exam	el examen
exam (pre-university)	el bachillerato
to **examine**	examinar
excellent	excelente
exchange	el intercambio
to **excuse**	perdonar
Excuse me!	¡Perdón!
exercise	el ejercicio
exercise book	el cuaderno
exhausted	agotado
to **exist**	existir
exit	la salida
explanation	la explicación
express train	el expreso; el rápido
extraordinary	extraordinario
eye	el ojo

	face	la cara; el rostro
	factory	la fábrica
to	fail	fracasar
to	fail (in an exam)	suspender
to	faint	desmayarse
	fair	la feria
to	fall	caer
to	fall asleep	dormirse
	false	falso
	family	la familia
	famous	célebre; famoso
	fan (lady's)	el abanico
	fantastic	fantástico
at the	far end	al fondo
	far from	lejos de
	farm	la finca; la granja
	farmer	el granjero
	fashion	la moda
	fast	rápido
to	fasten your seat-belt	abrocharse el cinturón
	fat	gordo
	father	el padre
	father-in-law	el suegro
	favourite	favorito
	fear	el miedo
	fed up	harto
to	feel	sentir (se)
to	feel sick	marearse
	feeling ill	mareado
	feminine	femenino
	ferry	el ferry
	festival	la fiesta
	few	pocos
	field (sports)	el campo (de deportes)

fifth	quinto
fig	el higo
to **fight**	luchar; pelear
fight	la pelea
to **fight** bulls	torear
figure (number)	la cifra
to **fill**	llenar; rellenar
filling (in tooth)	el empaste
film (e.g. at cinema)	la película
to **find**	encontrar; hallar
fine (i.e. money)	la multa
finger	el dedo
to **finish**	acabar; terminar
fire	el fuego; el incendio; la lumbre (hearth)
fireman	el bombero
firm (i.e. company)	la empresa
first	primero
first aid	primeros auxilios (*m*)
first name	el nombre de pila
first performance	el estreno
fish (when alive)	el pez
fish (when dead)	el pescado
fisherman	el pescador
fishing rod	la caña de pescar
fishmonger	el pescadero
fishmonger's (shop)	la pescadería
fit (of coughing)	el acceso (de tos)
fitting room	el probador
to **fix** (punctures)	arreglar (pinchazos)
flag	la bandera
flat (e.g. pancake)	llano
flat (i.e. apartment)	el piso
flat roof	la azotea
flavour	el sabor

flight	el vuelo
the second **floor**	el segundo piso
floor (of a room)	el suelo
flour	la harina
flower	la flor
flowerpot	la maceta
fly	la mosca
to **fly**	volar
fog	la neblina; la niebla
folding chair	la silla plegable
to **follow**	seguir
following	siguiente
food	el alimento; los comestibles
fool	el imbécil
foot	el pie
football	el fútbol
footballer	el futbolista
for	para
for example	por ejemplo
to **force**	forzar
forehead	la frente
foreign	extranjero
to **forget**	olvidar
fork	el tenedor
form	la ficha
fortnight	quince días
fortress	el alcázar
fortunate	afortunado
fortunately	afortunadamente
Forward!	¡Adelante!
fountain	la fuente; el surtidor
free (no charge; unoccupied)	libre

the meal *la comida*

free (no charge)	gratis; gratuito
free time	los ratos libres
to **freeze**	congelar
to **freeze**	helar
freezer	el congelador
French/France	francés/Francia (*f*)
fresh	fresco
fridge	la nevera
fried	frito
friend	el amigo/la amiga; el compañero/la compañera
friendly	amistoso
friendship	la amistad
fright	el susto
fritter	el churro
from	desde
from	a partir de
from time to time	de vez en cuando
in **front** of	delante de
frost	la escarcha
frozen food	alimentos congelados (*m*)
fruit	la fruta
fruit store	la frutería
fruit-seller	el frutero
frying pan	la sartén
full	completo; lleno
full board	pensión completa (*f*)
funny	divertido; gracioso
furious	furioso
furnished	amueblado
furniture	los muebles
future	futuro
the **future**	el porvenir

game	el juego
gaol	la cárcel
garage	el garaje
garden	el jardín
gardener	el jardinero
gardening	la jardinería
garlic	el ajo
garlic sausage	el chorizo
gas cooker	la cocina de gas
in general	por lo general
generous	generoso
gentleman	el caballero
geography	la geografía
German/Germany	alemán/Alemania (*f*)
to get	coger
to get information	informarse
to get up	levantarse
to get up early	madrugar
girl	la chica; la muchacha; la niña
girlfriend	la novia
to give	dar
to give a present	regalar
to give back	devolver
to give way (at junction)	ceder el paso
glass	el vaso
glass (material)	el vidrio
glass of beer	la caña
glasses (spectacles)	las gafas
glove	el guante
to go	ir
to go away	alejarse; irse; marcharse
to go camping	ir de camping

to **go** down	bajar
to **go** for a sail	dar un paseo en barco de vela
to **go** for a stroll	dar un paseo; dar una vuelta
to **go** out	salir
to **go** shopping	hacer compras
to **go** to (an appointment)	acudir a (una cita)
to **go** to bed	acostarse
to **go** up	subir
goat	la cabra
God	Dios (*m*)
gold	el oro
good	bueno
it is **good** weather	hace buen tiempo
goodbye	adiós
Gosh!	¡Caramba! ¡Madre mia!
government	el gobierno
graduate	el licenciado
grammar	la gramática
gram(me)	el gramo
grandfather/mother	el abuelo/abuela
grandson/daughter	el nieto/la nieta
grant	la beca
grape	la uva
grass	la hierba
to **grasp**	coger
grateful	agradecido
Great Britain	Gran Bretaña (*f*)
Greek/Greece	griego/Grecia (*f*)
green	verde
to **greet**	saludar
greetings	los saludos
grey	gris
ground	la tierra

	ground floor	la planta baja
	group	el grupo
to	**grow**	crecer
to	**grow** (e.g. vegetables)	cultivar
to	**guarantee**	garantizar
	guard (on train)	el revisor
	guest	el huésped; el invitado
	guide (book)	la guía
	guide (person)	el guía
	guinea-pig	el cobayo
	guitar	la guitarra
	gym (building)	el gimnasio
	gymnastics	la gimnasia

_____   _____
_____   _____
_____   _____

hair	el cabello
hair	el pelo
hair dryer	el secador
hairdresser (person)	el peluquero
hairdresser (place)	la peluquería
hake	la merluza
half	medio
half	la mitad
half-board	media pensión
hall (in a house)	el vestíbulo
ham	el jamón
hamburger	la hamburguesa

hamster	el hamster
hand	la mano
handbag	el bolso de mano
handkerchief	el pañuelo
handsome	guapo
to hang	colgar
to happen	ocurrir; pasar; suceder
happiness	la alegría
happy	alegre; contento; feliz
hard	duro
hard-working	trabajador
harvest	la cosecha
hat	el sombrero
to hate	detestar; odiar
to have	haber; tener
to have a good (bad) time	pasarlo bien (mal)
to have just (eaten)	acabar de (comer)
to have to	deber; tener que
head	la cabeza
to head for	dirigirse
have a headache	me duele la cabeza
headlight	el faro
headmaster	el director
health	la salud
to hear	oír
heart	el corazón
to heat	calentar
heat	el calor
heating	la calefacción
heavy	pesado
hedge	el seto
heel	el tacón
height	la altura
helicopter	el helicóptero

	Hello	Hola
	Hello! (answering phone)	¡Dígame!
	help	la ayuda
to	**help**	ayudar
	Help!	¡Socorro!
	hen	la gallina
	here	aquí
to	**hesitate**	dudar; vacilar
to	**hide**	esconder
	high	alto
	hill	la colina
to	**hire**	alquilar
	history	la historia
to	**hit**	golpear; pegar
	hitch-hiker	el/la autostopista
	hitch-hiking	el autostop
to go	**hitch-hiking**	hacer autostop
	hobby	la afición
	hold-up (robbery)	el atraco
	hole	el agujero
	holiday	el día festivo
	holidays	las vacaciones
	Holland	la Holanda
	Holy Week	la Semana Santa
	home	el hogar
	homework	los deberes
	honeymoon	la luna de miel
	hooligan	el gamberro
to	**hope**	esperar
	horrible	horrible
	horror film	la película de mied
	horse	el caballo
	horse-riding	la equitación
	hospital	el hospital
	hot	caliente; caluroso
to be	**hot** weather	hacer calor

hotel	el hotel
hotel (government-run)	el parador
hour	la hora
house	la casa
housewife	la ama de casa
how?	¿cómo?
How are you?	¿Qué tal?
How horrible!	¡Qué horror!
how much?	¿Cuánto?
How nice!	¡Qué bien!
however	no obstante; sin embargo
hundred	cien(to)
hunger	la hambre
to hunt	cazar
hunting	la caza
to hurt	doler
husband	el esposo; el marido

_____ _____
_____ _____
_____ _____
_____ _____
_____ _____

BCDEFGH**I**JKLMNOPQRSTUVWXYZ

ice	el hielo
ice-cream	el helado
ideal	ideal
identity card	el carnet de identidad
idiot	el idiota
if	si

ill	enfermo
illness	la enfermedad
immediately	inmediatamente
immense	inmenso
importance	la importancia
important	importante
impossible	imposible
to improve	mejorar
incapable	incapaz
included	incluido
to increase	aumentar
industry	la industria
influenza	la gripe
information	la información; los informes
inhabitant	el habitante
injection	la inyección
to injure	herir
injured	herido
inn	la fonda
innocent	inocente
insect	el insecto
to insert (coins)	introducir (monedas)
inside	adentro; dentro de
inspector	el inspector
instant	el instante
instrument	el instrumento
insufficient	insuficiente
insurance	el seguro
intelligent	inteligente
intention	la intención
interest	el interés
interesting	interesante
interior	interior
international	internacional

to **interpret**	interpretar
to **introduce**	presentar
invitation	la invitación
to **invite**	convidar; invitar
Irish/Ireland	irlandés/Irlanda (f)
iron (metal)	el hierro
to **iron**	planchar
island	la isla
isolated	aislado
Italian/Italy	italiano/Italia (f)
the school	
itself	el colegio mismo

_____ _____
_____ _____
_____ _____
_____ _____

ABCDEFGHI**J**KLMNOPQRSTUVWXYZ

jacket	la chaqueta
jersey	el jersey
jewel	la alhaja; la joya
jeweller's (shop)	la joyería
job	el empleo
joke	el chiste
journalist	el/la periodista
journey	el viaje
judge	el juez
to **judge**	juzgar
juice	el jugo; el zumo
to **jump**	saltar

to **keep**	guardar
Keep the change!	¡Quédese con la vuelta!
key	la llave
to **kidnap**	secuestrar
kidnapping	el secuestro
to **kill**	matar
kilogram(me)	el kilo
kilometre	el kilómetro
king	el rey
kiosk	el quiosco
to **kiss**	besar
kiss	el beso
kitchen	la cocina
knee	la rodilla
knickers	las bragas
knife	el cuchillo
knife, fork and spoon	el cubierto
to **knit**	hacer punto
to **knock** down	atropellar
to **know** (a person or place)	conocer
to **know** (something)	saber

_____ _____

_____ _____

_____ _____

laboratory	el laboratorio
lack	la falta
to **lack**	faltar

lake	el lago
lamb	el cordero
lame	cojo
lamp	la lámpara
to land (a plane)	aterrizar
landing (of a plane)	el aterrizaje
language	el idioma; la lengua
to last	durar
last	último
last Monday	el lunes pasado
last night	anoche
last year	el año pasado
at last	por fin
late	tarde
to laugh	reír
laughter	la risa
lawn	el césped
lawyer	el abogado
to lay the table	poner la mesa
lazy	perezoso
lead (metal)	el plomo
leader	el líder
leaf	la hoja
to learn	aprender
leather	el cuero
to leave a place	dejar un sitio
to the left	a la izquierda
left-luggage office	la consigna
leg	la pierna
lemon	el limón
lemonade	la gaseosa; la limonada
to lend	prestar
lenses (contact)	las lentillas
less	menos

lesson	la clase; la lección
to **let**	dejar
letter (i.e. post)	la carta
letter (of alphabet)	la letra
letter-box	el buzón
lettuce	la lechuga
level	el nivel
level crossing	el paso a nivel
liberty	la libertad
library	la biblioteca
lie	la mentira
to **lie down**	tenderse; tumbars
life	la vida
lift (elevator)	el ascensor
to **light**	encender
light	la luz
light (not heavy)	ligero
lightning	el relámpago
line	la fila; la línea
lion	el león
lip	el labio
liquid	el líquido
list	la lista
to **listen**	escuchar
Listen!	¡Oiga!
literature	la literatura
litre	el litro
little (not much)	poco
a **little** after one o'clock	a la una y pico
a **lot**	mucho
to **live**	vivir
living-room	la sala de estar
loaf	la barra
lobster	la langosta
lock	la cerradura

to **lock**	cerrar con llave
lodgings	el alojamiento
London	Londres (*m*)
lonely	solitario
long	largo
to **look** after	cuidar
to **look** at	mirar
to **look** for	buscar
to **look** out (e.g. of window)	asomarse
lorry	el camión
to **lose**	perder
loss	la pérdida
lost-property office	la oficina de objetos perdidos
a **lot**	mucho
lottery	la lotería
lounge	el salón
love	el amor
in **love**	enamorado
luck	la suerte
luggage	el equipaje
lukewarm	tibio
to **lunch**	almorzar
lunch	el almuerzo
luxury	el lujo
luxury hotel	el hotel de lujo

machine	la máquina
mad	loco
magazine	la revista
magnificent	magnífico
maid	la criada
main course	el plato principal
main door	la puerta principa
to **maintain**	mantener
majority	la mayoría
make (e.g. of car)	la marca
to **make** a mistake	equivocarse
to **make** noise	hacer ruido
to **make** the bed	hacer la cama
make-up	el maquillaje
man	el hombre
to **manage** (to do something)	lograr; llegar a
manager	el gerente
to **manufacture**	fabricar
map (e.g. of roads)	el mapa
map (e.g. of a city)	el plano
mark (e.g. in an exam)	la nota
market	el mercado
marmalade	la mermelada
married	casado
married couple	el matrimonio
to **marry**	casarse
masculine	masculino
mass (religious service)	la misa
match (e.g. football)	el partido
match (for a fire)	la cerilla
maths	las matemáticas
it doesn't	
matter	no importa
mattress	el colchón
maximum	máximo
mayonnaise	la mayonesa

mayor	el alcalde
meadow	el prado
meal	la comida
to mean	querer decir; significar
meanwhile	entretanto
to measure	medir
meat	la carne
meatball	la albóndiga
mechanic	el mecánico
medicine	la medicina
the Mediterranean	el Mediterráneo
medium	mediano
to meet a friend	encontrar a un amigo
meeting	la reunión
melon	el melón
member	el miembro
memory	el recuerdo
menu	el menú
menu for tourists	el menú turístico
menu of the day	el menú del día
message	el recado
metal	el metal
metre	el metro
midday	el mediodía
about the middle of	a mediados de
midnight	la medianoche
milk	la leche
milkman	el lechero
mine	la mina
miner	el minero
mineral water (fizzy)	la agua mineral (con gas)
mineral water (still)	la agua mineral (sin gas)

minimum	mínimo
minority	la minoría
minute	el minuto
mirror	el espejo
to miss (someone)	echar de menos
mistake	el error
model	el modelo
modern	moderno
moment	el momento
for the moment	por ahora
money	el dinero
monkey	el mono
month	el mes
monthly	mensual
monument	el monumento
moon	la luna
more	más
in the morning	por la mañana
mother	la madre
mother-in-law	la suegra
motionless	inmóvil
motorbike	la moto
motorway	la autopista
mountain	la montaña; el monte
mountainous	montañoso
mouse	el ratón
moustache	el bigote
mouth	la boca
move (i.e. house)	la mudanza
to move	mover; trasladar
to move house	mudarse
moving (emotionally)	emocionante
mud	el barro
Mummy	Mamá
to murder	asesinar

murder	el asesinato
museum	el museo
mushrooms	los champiñones
music	la música
musician	el músico
mussel	el mejillón
mustard	la mostaza
mute	mudo
mysterious	misterioso

_____   _____
_____   _____
_____   _____
_____   _____
_____   _____

BCDEFGHIJKLM**N**OPQRSTUVWXYZ

name	el nombre
nap	la siesta
narrow	estrecho
nation	la nación
nationality	la nacionalidad
native (of a country)	natural
naughty	travieso
nausea	el mareo
near	cerca de
nearby	cercano
necessary	necesario; preciso
it is **necessary**	hace falta; hay que
neck	el cuello
necklace	el collar
to **need**	necesitar
needle	la aguja
neighbour	el vecino/la vecina

neighbourhood	la vecindad
neither	tampoco
neither ... nor	ni ... ni ...
nephew	el sobrino
nervous	nervioso
net	la red
netball	la balonred
the **Netherlands**	Holanda (*f*)
never	jamás; nunca
new	nuevo
New Year's Eve	la Nochevieja
the **news**	las noticias
newspaper	el periódico
next	próximo
next to	junto a
next year	el año próximo (qu viene)
nice (of people)	simpático
niece	la sobrina
night	la noche
no	ninguno
No entry	Prohibido el paso
nobody	nadie
noise	el ruido
noisy	ruidoso
normal	normal
the **north**	el norte
nose	la nariz
note (e.g. in a notebook)	el apunte
notebook	la agenda; la libre
nothing	nada
notice	el aviso; el letrero
novel	la novela
now	ahora; ya
nurse	la enfermera

to **obey**	obedecer
object	el objeto
to **obtain**	conseguir; obtener
octopus	el pulpo
of course!	¡claro!
offence	el delito
offer	la oferta
to **offer**	ofrecer
office	el despacho; la oficina
official	oficial
official	el oficial
often	a menudo
oil	el aceite
Okay?	¿Vale?
old	anciano; viejo
olive	la aceituna
omelette	la tortilla
on	sobre; en
one o'clock	
on the dot	a la una en punto
on the point of	a punto de
onion	la cebolla
only (i.e. just)	solamente
only (alone)	sólo; único
open	abierto
to **open**	abrir
be in the	
open air	estar al aire libre
operation	la operación
opinion	la opinión
opportunity	la oportunidad
opposite	enfrente
or	o/u
orange	la naranja
orangeade	la naranjada

orchestra	la orquesta
to **organize**	organizar
origin	el origen
other	otro
our	nuestro
out of order	no funciona
outing	la excursión
outside	afuera; fuera
outsider	el forastero
outskirts	las afueras
outstanding	sobresaliente
oven	el horno
to **overtake**	adelantar
to **owe**	deber
my **own** house	mi propia casa
owner	el dueño; el propietario

_____   _____

_____   _____

_____   _____

packet	el paquete
page	la página
pain	el dolor
to **paint**	pintar
painter	el pintor
painting	la pintura
pair	el par
palace	el palacio
pale	pálido
paper	el papel

parents	los padres
to park	aparcar; estacionar
part	la parte
party (get-together)	la fiesta particular
to pass (an exam)	aprobar
passenger	el pasajero
passer-by	el transeúnte
passport	el pasaporte
the past	el pasado
pastime	el pasatiempo
path	el sendero
patrol	la patrulla
pavement	la acera
to pay	pagar
payment	el pago
peace	la paz
peach	el melocotón
pear	la pera
pear tree	el peral
pearl	la perla
peas	los guisantes
peasant	el campesino
pedestrian	el peatón
pedestrian crossing	el paso de peatones
pencil	el lápiz
peninsula	la península
people	la gente
pepper (white)	la pimienta
pepper (e.g. red)	el pimiento
per cent	por ciento
perfect	perfecto
performance (at cinema)	la sesión
perfume	el perfume
perhaps	quizá(s); tal vez
period of time	la época
person	la persona

to **persuade**	persuadir
petrol	la gasolina
petrol (high-grade)	súper
petrol (low-grade)	normal
petrol tank	el depósito
petrol station	la gasolinera
to **phone**	llamar por teléfono
phone call	la conferencia; la llamada
photo(graph)	la foto(grafía)
photographer	el fotógrafo
physics	la fisica
piano	el piano
pickpocket	el ratero
to **picnic**	merendar
picnic	la merienda
picture	el cuadro
piece	el pedazo; el trozo
pig	el cerdo
pillow	la almohada
pilot	el aviador; el piloto
pin	el alfiler
pineapple	la piña
pipe	la pipa
pistol	la pistola
What a **pity!**	¡Qué lástima!
to **place**	colocar
place	el lugar; el sitio
plan	el proyecto
plane	el avión
plant	la planta
plate	el plato
platform (on station)	el andén
to **play**	jugar
play (at theatre)	la obra de teatro
to **play** the guitar	tocar la guitarra

pleasant	agradable; amable
please	por favor
to please	gustar
pleased to meet you	encantado
plum	la ciruela
pocket	el bolsillo
to point	indicar
police	la policía
police station	la comisaría
policeman	el guardia; el policía
polite	cortés
politely	atentamente
pond	el estanque
poor	pobre
pop music	la música pop
population	la población
port	el puerto
porter	el mozo
portion	la ración
Portuguese/Portugal	portugués/Portugal (m)
to possess	poseer
possible	posible
postcard	la postal
postman	el cartero
post office	correos (m)
poster	el cartel
pothole (in road)	el bache
potato	la patata
pound (sterling)	la libra (esterlina)
to pour with rain	llover a cántaros
poverty	la pobreza
to practice	practicar
prawn	la gamba; la langostina
precise	preciso

to **prefer**	preferir
pregnant	embarazada
to **prepare**	preparar
present (i.e. gift)	el regalo
at **present**	actualmente
the **press**	la prensa
pretty	bonito; guapa; lind●
to **prevent**	impedir
previous	anterior
price	el precio
price list	la tarifa
priest	el cura; el sacerdote
private	particular
prize	el premio
problem	el problema
procession	la procesión
programme	el programa
to **prohibit**	prohibir
to **promise**	prometer
to **protect**	proteger
proud	orgulloso
province	la provincia
to **pull**	tirar
puncture	el pinchazo
to **punish**	castigar
punishment	el castigo
pupil	el alumno/la alumna
to **pursue**	perseguir
to **push**	empujar
to **put**	meter; poner
to **put** up with	aguantar
to **put** up (a tent)	armar (una tienda)
pyjamas	el pijama
the **Pyrenees**	los Pireneos

quality	la calidad
quantity	la cantidad
quarter (of an hour)	el cuarto (de hora)
queen	la reina
question	la pregunta
queue	la cola
to be **quiet**	callarse

_____ _____

_____ _____

_____ _____

_____ _____

rabbit	el conejo
radiator	el radiador
radio	la radio
railway	el ferrocarril
to **rain**	llover
rain	la lluvia
raincoat	el impermeable
rainstorm	el aguacero
range of mountains	la sierra
raspberry	la frambuesa
rat	la rata
rather	más bien
rather (small)	algo (pequeño)
to **read**	leer
reading	la lectura
to be **ready**	estar listo
to **realize**	darse cuenta
reason	la razón
receipt	el recibo

receiver (telephone)	el auricular
to receive (money)	cobrar (dinero)
to receive	recibir
recent(ly)	reciente(mente)
reception (in hotel)	la recepción
receptionist	el/la recepcionista
recipe	la receta
to recognize	reconocer
to recommend	recomendar
record (music)	el disco
record-player	el tocadiscos
red	rojo
red wine	el vino tinto
red-haired	pelirrojo
reduction	la rebaja
referee	el árbitro
refreshment (soft drink)	el refresco
to refuse	negarse a
region	la región
registration (of a car)	la matrícula
relatives	los parientes
religion	la religión
remedy	el remedio
to remember	acordarse; recordar
rent	el alquiler
repair	la reparación
to repair	reparar
to repeat	repetir
reply	la respuesta
to report to the police	denunciar
representative	el/la representante
to rescue	rescatar
rescue	el rescate
to resemble	parecerse a
to reserve	reservar
residence	el domicilio

responsible	responsable
to **rest**	descansar
rest	el descanso
the **rest** (i.e. the remainder)	lo demás
restaurant	el restaurante
to **retire**	jubilarse
retired	jubilado
return	la vuelta
to **return**	regresar; volver
return ticket	el billete de ida y vuelta
to **revise** (for exams)	repasar
reward	la recompensa
rice	el arroz
rich	rico
to **ride** (horses)	montar a caballo
rifle	el fusil
on the **right**	a la derecha
ring (on finger)	el anillo; la sortija
risk	el riesgo
river	el río
road (between towns)	la carretera
to **roast**	asar
roast chicken	el pollo asado
rock music	la música rock
roll (bread)	el panecillo
roof	el tejado
room	el cuarto; la habitación
a **room** available	la habitación libre
Is there any **room**?	¿Hay sitio?
rosé wine	el vino rosado
round	redondo
routine	la rutina
to **row** (a boat)	remar

rubber	la goma
rubbish	la basura
rucksack	la mochila
rug	la alfombrilla
rule(r)	la regla
rum	el ron
to run	correr
to run away	huir
to run out of	agotarse
running (water)	corriente
rush hour	la hora punta
Russian/Russia	ruso/Rusia (f)

_____ _____

_____ _____

_____ _____

ABCDEFGHIJKLMNOPQR**S**TUVWXYZ

sad	triste
safe and sound	sano y salvo
safety-belt	el cinturón de seguridad
sail	la vela
sailor	el marinero
saint	el santo
salad	la ensalada
salary	el sueldo
sale	la venta
salt	la sal
same	igual
the same school	el mismo colegio
sand	la arena
sandal	la sandalia
sandwich	el bocadillo
sardine	la sardina

to **satisfy**	satisfacer
sauce	la salsa
saucepan	la cacerola
saucer	el platillo
sausage	la salchicha
sausage (large) (salami)	el salchichón
to **save** (e.g. from danger)	salvar
to **save** (money)	ahorrar
savings bank	la caja de ahorros
to **say**	decir
to **say** goodbye to	despedirse
scarcely	apenas
school	el colegio; la escuela; el instituto
science	la ciencia
science-fiction	la ciencia-ficción
scissors	las tijeras
to **score** a goal	marcar un gol
Scottish/Scotland	escocés/Escocia (f)
screen	la pantalla
sea	el/la mar
to **search**	registrar
at the **seaside**	a orillas del mar
season of the year	la estación del año
seat	el asiento
seat (e.g. in a cinema)	la localidad
second	el segundo
secretary	el secretario/la secretaria
section	la sección
to **see**	ver
to **seem**	parecer
to **seize**	agarrar
to **sell**	vender
seller (of goods)	el vendedor
to **send**	enviar; mandar

	sentence (words)	la frase
	serious	grave; serio
to	serve	servir
	service	el servicio
	service station	la estación de servicios
	serviette	servilleta
	seventh	séptimo
	several	varios
to	sew	coser
	shadow	la sombra
	shampoo	el champú
	shape	la forma
to	share	compartir
	sharp	agudo
to	shave	afeitarse
	sheep	la oveja
	sheet (on bed)	la sábana
	sheet of paper	la hoja de papel
	shellfish	los mariscos
	sherry	el jerez
to	shine	brillar
	ship	el buque
	shirt	la camisa
to	shiver	tiritar
	shoe	el zapato
	shoemaker	el zapatero
	shoeshine boy	el limpiabotas
	shoe shop	la zapatería
	shop (large)	el almacén
	shop	la tienda
	shop assistant	el/la dependiente/a
	shop window	el escaparate
	shopkeeper	el tendero
to go	shopping	ir de compras
	short	corto

short while	el rato
shorthand	la taquigrafía
shoulder	el hombro
to **shout**	gritar
show	el espectáculo
to **show**	mostrar
shower (of rain)	el chubasco
shower (in bathroom)	la ducha
shy	tímido
sideboard	el aparador
side-street	la bocacalle
to **sign**	firmar
sign	la señal
signature	la firma
silence	el silencio
silent	silencioso
silk	la seda
silly	necio
silver	la plata
similar	parecido; semejante
simple	sencillo
since (because)	puesto que; ya que
to **sing**	cantar
singer	el/la cantante
single bed	la cama individual
single room	la habitación individual
single ticket	el billete sencillo (de ida)
sister	la hermana
sister-in-law	la cuñada
to **sit** down	sentarse
situated	situado
sixth	sexto
size	el tamaño
size (of a person)	la talla
skate (for ice)	el patín

to **skate**	patinar
skating	el patinaje
skating rink	la pista de patinaje
to **ski**	esquiar
skiing	el esquí
skin	la piel
skirt	la falda
sky	el cielo
to **sleep**	dormir
sleeping bag	el saco de dormir
sleeping car (on train)	el coche-cama
sleeve	la manga
slice (of meat)	la lonja
to **slip**	resbalar
slipper	la zapatilla
slope	la pendiente
slow	lento
slowly	despacio; lentamente
small	pequeño
small letter	la minúscula
smaller	menor
to **smell**	oler
smell	el olor
to **smile**	sonreír
smile	la sonrisa
to **smoke**	fumar
smoke	el humo
smuggler	el contrabandista
snake	la culebra
to **snow**	nevar
snow	la nieve
so (happy)	tan (contento)
so much	tanto
so so!	¡así así!
so that	así que

soaked	mojado
to get **soaked**	mojarse
soaked to the skin	mojado hasta los huesos
soap	el jabón
sock	el calcetín
sofa	el sofá
soft	suave
soldier	el soldado
sole (fish)	el lenguado
some	alguno; unos/unas
someone	alguien
something	algo
sometimes	a veces
son	el hijo
song	la canción
soon	pronto
as **soon** as possible	cuanto antes
to **sound**	sonar
soup	la sopa
soup (cold)	el gazpacho
the **south**	el sur
South America	América del Sur (*f*)
spade	la pala
Spanish cooking	la cocina española
Spanish/Spain	español/España (*f*)
Spanish Railways	RENFE
spare wheel	la rueda de repuesto
Speaking! (on phone)	¡Al aparato!
speed	la prisa; la velocidad
to **spend** (money)	gastar
to **spend** (time)	pasar
to **spend** the summer	veranear
spinach	las espinacas
spinster	la soltera
in **spite** of	a pesar de

	splendid	estupendo
	spoon	la cuchara
	sport	el deporte
	sporting	deportivo
	sportsman/woman	el/la deportista
	spring (season)	la primavera
	square (in a town)	la plaza
	squid	el calamar
	stadium	el estadio
	stain	la mancha
	stairs	la escalera
	stamp	el sello
	star	la estrella
to	**start** (a car)	arrancar
	starter (in a restaurant)	el entremés
	station	la estación
	stationer's shop	la papelería
	statue	la estatua
to	**stay**	permanecer; quedar
to	**stay** in bed	guardar cama
	steak	el biftec/bistec
to	**steal**	robar
	steel	el acero
	steering wheel	el volante
	step	el paso
	stew	el cocido
	still	aún; todavía
	stocking	la media
	stomach	el estómago
	stone	la piedra
	stool	el taburete
to	**stop**	detenerse; pararse
	Stop!	¡Alto!
	storm	la borrasca; la tempestad; la tormenta

straight on	todo derecho; todo recto; todo seguido
strange	extraño; raro
straw	la paja
strawberry	la fresa
street	la calle
street (main)	la calle mayor
street (small)	la callejuela
strict	severo
strike	la huelga
stroll	el paseo
strong	fuerte
struggle	la lucha
student	el/la estudiante
studies	los estudios
studiousness	la aplicación
to **study**	estudiar
stupid	estúpido; tonto
subject (at school)	la asignatura
subscriber	el abonado
to **substitute**	sustituir
suburb	el suburbio
success	el éxito
such a person	tal persona
sudden	súbito
suddenly	de repente
suede	el ante
to **suffer**	sufrir
sugar	el azúcar
to **suggest**	proponer
suit (of clothes)	el traje
suitcase	la maleta
summer	el verano
sun	el sol
sunglasses	las gafas de sol

sunstroke	la insolación
suntan cream	la loción bronceadora
sunshade	el parasol
supermarket	el supermercado
supplement	el suplemento
to **suppose**	suponer
sure	seguro
surname	el apellido
surprise	la sorpresa
suspicious	sospechoso
to **swallow**	tragar
to **swear**	jurar
to **sweat**	sudar
to **sweep**	barrer
sweet	el caramelo; el dulce
sweet	dulce
sweet (made from almonds)	el turrón
to **swell**	hincharse
to **swim**	nadar
swimming	la natación
swimming costume	el bañador; el traje de baño
swimming pool	la piscina
swing (child's)	el columpio
Swiss/Switzerland	suizo/Suiza (f)
to **switch** off (e.g. a light)	apagar
swollen	hinchado
symptom	el síntoma

table	la mesa
table tennis	el ping-pong
tablecloth	el mantel
tablet	la pastilla
tailor	el sastre
to take	tomar
to take (a person)	llevar
to take lodgings	alojarse
to take notice	hacer caso
to take off (a plane)	despegar
to take off (clothes)	quitar(se)
to take out (i.e. extract)	sacar
to take place	tener lugar
to take time (to do)	tardar
to take your fancy	apetecer
to talk	hablar
talkative	hablador
to tan (in the sun)	broncearse
tap	el grifo
tart	la tarta
task	la tarea
taste	el gusto
tavern	la taberna
tax	el impuesto
taxi	el taxi
taxi driver	el taxista
tea	el té
to teach	enseñar
teacher	el maestro; el profesor
teaching	la enseñanza
team	el equipo
teapot	la tetera
tear (in your eye)	la lágrima
telegram	el telegrama
telephone box	la cabina telefónica

telephone book	la guía telefónica
telephone number	el número de teléfono
to **telephone**	telefonear
telephone	el teléfono
television	la televisión
television set	el televisor
to **tell** (a story)	contar
temperature (fever)	la fiebre
temperature	la temperatura
tennis	el tenis
tent	la tienda (de campaña)
term (e.g. at school)	el trimestre
terrible	terrible
terrorist	el/la terrorista
test	la prueba
to **thank** for	agradecer
Thank goodness!	¡Menos mal!
thank you	gracias
that	aquel/aquella; ese/esa
theatre	el teatro
then	entonces; luego; pues
there	ahí; allá; allí
there is; there are	hay
therefore	por lo tanto
thermometer	el termómetro
these	estos/estas
thick	espeso; grueso
thief	el ladrón
thin	delgado; flaco
thing	la cosa
to **think**	pensar
to **think** (hold an opinion)	opinar

third	tercero
thirst	la sed
this	este/esta
those	aquellos/aquellas; esos/esas
thread	el hilo
to threaten	amenazar
throat	la garganta
through (train)	directo
to throw	arrojar; echar; lanzar
to thunder	tronar
thunder	el trueno
ticket	el billete
ticket office	la taquilla
ticket clerk	el taquillero
tide	la marea
to tidy (the house)	arreglar (la casa)
to tie	atar
tie (that you wear)	la corbata
tiger	el tigre
tile	el azulejo
time (occasion)	la vez
timetable	el horario
tin	la lata
tin-opener	el abrelatas
tip (money)	la propina
tired	cansado
title	el título
toast	el pan tostado
tobacco	el tabaco
tobacconist	el estanco; la tabacelera
today	hoy
toilet	el aseo; el retrete; el wáter

	toilet paper	el papel higiénico
	toilets	los servicios
to	tolerate	tolerar
	toll (on motorway)	el peaje
	tomato	el tomate
	tomorrow	mañana
	tomorrow morning	mañana por la mañana
	tongue	la lengua
	too much	demasiado
	tooth	el diente
	tooth (a molar)	la muela
	toothpaste	la pasta de dientes
a	toothpick	el palillo
	top	la cima
the	top (of a mountain)	la cumbre
	torch	la linterna
to	touch	tocar
	tourist	el/la turista
	tourist menu	el menú turístico
	tourist office	la oficina de turism
	towards	hacia
	towel	la toalla
	tower	la torre
	town	el pueblo
	town hall	el ayuntamiento
	toy	el juguete
	track (railway)	la vía
	trader	el comerciante
	trades union	el sindicato
	traffic	el tráfico
	traffic jam	el embotellamiento
	traffic lights	los semáforos
	tragedy	la tragedia
	train	el tren
	train (special service)	TALGO

tram	el tranvía
transistor (radio)	el transistor
to **translate**	traducir
to **travel**	viajar
travel agent	la agencia de viajes
traveller	el viajero
traveller's cheque	el cheque de viajero
tray	la bandeja
to **tread** on	pisar
treatment	el tratamiento
tree	el árbol
to **tremble**	temblar
trolley (in supermarket)	el carrito
pair of **trousers**	los pantalones
trout	la trucha
true	verdadero
truly	de veras
trunk (luggage)	el baúl
truth	la verdad
to **try**	intentar; procurar; tratar
to **try** out	probarse
to **use** 'tú'	tutear
turkey	el pavo
to **turn** (e.g. to the right)	torcer
to **turn** (the corner)	doblar (la esquina)
to **turn** round	volverse
turtle	la tortuga
twin	el gemelo
twin beds	camas gemelas (*f*)
to **type**	escribir a máquina
type	el tipo
typewriter	la máquina de escribir
typical	típico
typing	la mecanografía

typist	la mecanógrafa
tyre	el neumático

_____ _____
_____ _____
_____ _____

ugly	feo
umbrella	el paraguas
unacceptable	inaceptable
uncle	el tío
uncomfortable	incómodo
under	debajo de
underpants	los calzoncillos
to **understand**	comprender; entender
to **undress**	desnudarse
unemployed	desempleado
unemployed person	el parado
unemployment	el desempleo; el par
unfortunately	desafortunadamente; desgraciadamente
uniform	el uniforme
United States	los Estados Unidos
United Kingdom	el Reino Unido
university	la universidad
unjust	injusto
unpleasant	antipático; desagradable
unthinkable!	¡ni hablar!
until	hasta
untruthful	mentiroso

upstairs	arriba
urgent	urgente
to **use**	usar; utilizar
useful	útil
useless	inútil
to **usually** do something	soler

_____ _____

_____ _____

_____ _____

_____ _____

vacuum-cleaner	el aspirador; la aspiradora
valley	el valle
van	la camioneta
vase	el florero
VAT	IVA (impuesto sobre el valor añadido)
veal	la ternera
vegetable	la verdura
version	la versión
very	muy
video	el video
view	la vista
village	la aldea
villager	el aldeano
vinegar	el vinagre
violin	el violín
visit	la visita
to **visit**	visitar
voice	la voz
to **vomit**	vomitar

to **wait for**	aguardar; esperar
waiter	el camarero; el mozo
waiting-room	la sala de espera
to **wake up**	despertarse
to **walk**	andar
to go for a **walk**	pasearse
wall (inside)	la pared
wall (outside)	el muro; la tapia
wall (e.g. round a town)	la muralla
to **want**	desear; querer
to **want to**	tener ganas de
war	la guerra
wardrobe	el armario; el guardarropa
to **warn**	avisar
to **wash**	lavar
to **wash the dishes**	fregar los platos
to **wash yourself**	lavarse
washbasin	el lavabo
washing-machine	la lavadora automática
wasp	la avispa
watch	el reloj
watchmaker's (shop)	la relojería
water	agua (*f*)
to **water**	regar
water sports	los deportes acuáticos
to go **water-skiing**	hacer el esquí acuático
wave (sea)	la ola
to **wave** (your handkerchief)	agitar (el pañuelo)
way	el camino
way (of doing something)	la manera; el modo
weak	débil; flojo

to **wear** (clothes)	llevar (ropa)
weather	el tiempo
weather forecast	el pronóstico del tiempo; el boletín meteorológico
wedding	la boda
week	la semana
weekend	el fin de semana
to **weigh**	pesar
weight	el peso
welcome	bienvenido
well	bien
Welsh/Wales	galés/Gales (*f*)
the **west**	el oeste
western (film)	la película del oeste
what?	¿qué?
wheel	la rueda
when?	¿cuándo?
where?	¿dónde?
where to?	¿adónde?
which?	¿cuál?
while	mientras
whistle	el pito
to **whistle**	silbar
white	blanco
who	quien
whose	cuyo
why?	¿por qué?
wide	ancho
widow/widower	la viuda/el viudo
wife	la esposa; la mujer
wild	salvaje
to **win**	ganar
wind	el viento
window	la ventana
window (small)	la ventanilla

windscreen	el parabrisas
windscreen wipers	los limpiaparabri
wine	el vino
winter	el invierno
with	con
without	sin
witness	el testigo
woman	la mujer
to **wonder**	preguntarse
wonderful	precioso
wood (forest)	el bosque
wood (material)	la madera
wool	la lana
word	la palabra
work (of art)	la obra
work	el trabajo
to **work**	trabajar
worker	el obrero
working day	el día laborable
works (e.g. roadworks)	obras (*f*)
workshop	el taller
world	el mundo
worried	preocupado
to **worry**	inquietarse; preocuparse
worse	peor
it is **worth while**	vale la pena
wound	la herida
to **wrap up**	envolver
wrist	la muñeca
to **write**	escribir
writer	el/la escritor/a
wrong	incorrecto

yard (paved area)	el patio
year	el año
yellow	amarillo
yes	sí
yesterday	ayer
yogurt	el yogur
young	joven
youth club	el club de juventud
youth hostel	el albergue juvenil

_____   _____
_____   _____
_____   _____
_____   _____
_____   _____

zero	cero
zone	la zona
zoo	el zoo

_____   _____
_____   _____
_____   _____
_____   _____
_____   _____

algodón	cotton
seda	silk
lana	wool
lino	linen